WORSHIP
in the
GARDEN

WORSHIP
in the
GARDEN

SERVICES FOR OUTDOOR WORSHIP

J. WAYNE PRATT

Abingdon Press
NASHVILLE

WORSHIP *in the* GARDEN

Copyright © 2013 by J. Wayne Pratt

All rights reserved.

This book is printed on acid-free paper.

ISBN 978-1-426-76594-0

13 14 15 16 17 18 19 20 21 22—10 9 8 7 6 5 4 3 2 1

MANUFACTURED IN THE UNITED STATES OF AMERICA

CONTENTS

ACKNOWLEDGMENTS 1

FOREWORD 3

PREFACE 5

INTRODUCTION 7

BIBLICAL PRECEDENTS 11

LITURGIES 17

    Celebrating God's Creation 19

    Baptism of the Lord 35

    Baptismal Service 40

    Infant Dedication 47

    Congregational Reaffirmation
        of the Baptismal Covenant 52

    Communion 58

    Way of the Cross 63

    Easter Sunrise 81

    Blessing of the Animals 87

Healing Service 91

Reflection, Reconciliation, and Renewal 97

Love Feast 106

Wedding 113

Renewal of Wedding Vows 119

Memorial Service 123

Graveside Committal Service 127

LITURGICAL GARDENS: A RATIONALE 131

NOTES 136

ACKNOWLEDGMENTS

Two quite unique and special people came into my life a number of years ago. Both had a profound affect on my desire and ultimate decision to enter pastoral ministry. The Reverend Dr. Harold Brooks and the late Reverend Robert Craig unknowingly affected my life and faith journey in a variety of ways. Undoubtedly, I would not be where I am today had it not been for their keen influence and inspiration. It is my hope that this work will somehow serve as a thank you to them. Bless you both.

Professor Len Sweet of Drew Theological School—my mentor and my friend—I offer to you a very special gift of thanks for your ongoing inspiration and encouragement. Len, your prodding, pushing, and patience created a wonderful sense of excitement for discovery and participation in the many opportunities that God sends our way. You opened my eyes to God's Word in so many delightful new ways. I hold before me your gift of the ostrich egg as a bold and vibrant image statement. It serves as a constant reminder to me to keep my eyes focused on that which is good, lest it be lost. Thank you!

To my family, both intimate and extended, your support, encouragement, and patience in dealing with my quirks, quips, and qualms is both life-sustaining and empowering. May God bless you all.

FOREWORD

The Bible begins with a disquisition on dirt. At least that's where the micro creation account of Genesis 2 launches the birth story of the universe: no shrubs, no plants, just dirt and dust. When streams rise up from within and below, the surface of the ground is watered.

Wait a minute: when dirt and water mix, what do you get? Mud. Clay. How were you and I created? God, the Master Potter, scoops out of the ground a clump of clay, molds and makes it into the first human, and then breathes into that human the breath of God.

What is the earliest image of God in the Bible? God is playing in the dirt, making mud pies.

Maybe we shouldn't be so surprised that the soil contains friendly bacteria that affect the brain in a similar way to antidepressants. Scientists in the United Kingdom were the first to discover that bacteria commonly found in soil activated brain cells to produce the chemical serotonin, which acts as an antidepressant. Low levels of serotonin are linked with a number of disorders including aggression, anxiety, depression, obsessive-compulsive disorder (OCD), bipolar disorder, irritable bowel syndrome, and

fibromyalgia. Lead author of the study, Dr. Chris Lowry
from Bristol University, suggests that the research "leaves
us wondering if we shouldn't all be spending more time
playing in the dirt."[1] It also makes one wonder if this isn't
one reason many pregnant women crave clay and dirt?

In the macro creation account of Genesis 1, there is the
portrayal of God establishing the cosmos as God's temple,
meant to be filled and flooded with God's presence. On
day seven, God rests. "Rest" is a verb that is used almost
exclusively in ancient Near Eastern literature to describe
how God takes up residence in their temple.

But every temple needs a garden and every garden a
temple. In Genesis 2, the garden is a microcosm of the cosmos and God's mission for the macrocosm. Garden and
Temple—the two places that pinnacle and ritualize the
divine presence.

Wayne has written some marvelous liturgies and litanies
for our garden temples (and temple gardens) that cultivate
the soul during the diverse seasons of life—birth, baptism,
communion, wedding, funeral, and many rites of passage
in between. But be warned, *Worship in the Garden* is a
flowerbed of resources. You will need to get your hands
dirty and wet to use them. But don't clean your hands too
quickly. You don't want to wash away that "friendly bacteria" that keeps us healthy and whole.

Leonard Sweet
Drew University
George Fox University

PREFACE

In today's high-energy, busy, and often stressful world, an increasing number of people are yearning for a greater sense of inner peace. There also exists a deep and constant human longing to discover and understand the meaning of one's life. Spending time in a garden—any garden—has often been central to one's quest for greater spiritual discernment. A re-connection with the garden as a place where a divine presence dwells is the communal dream of many people.

References to gardens as oases of comfort or as metaphors for heaven or paradise are found in much of the sacred literature of the world's major religious traditions. Human beings are frequently searching to capture that image of a lost paradise in order to enjoy all of life's opportunities and pleasures.

In many religious traditions, the garden is a sacred place, ideal for establishing a greater connection with one's inner being. It is truly in the garden that one is able to discover an increased sense of peace and contentment through holy acts of prayer, dialogue, and relaxation. The tasks of prayer, meditation, and contemplation become much easier and more focused in a setting that provides a sense of connection with one's inner being and with a greater divine power. The "soul work" experienced in a garden setting is certainly conducive to emotional, physical, and spiritual healing and renewal.

The church has traditionally served as the "structure" to foster one's spiritual growth and development. In fact, the church building has often served as a principal focus of activity in the community, where a diverse mix of people has gathered in prayer and worship. The building itself typically has functioned as a place of sanctuary where a person may find solace and comfort, set apart from the intrusions and distractions of the world.

It is, however, in a garden where one's spiritual and emotional needs may be met in a simple and comfortable setting. The garden certainly may function as a vessel for liturgy and worship, offering enhanced opportunities for the gathering of people in what may be regarded as a neutral or comfort zone for faith experiences. Moreover, it is in the garden that one truly begins to discover and experience something greater than one's self—the creation and nurturing of human relationships that bind us together as people of faith.

INTRODUCTION

The kiss of the sun for pardon
The song of the birds for mirth
One is nearer to God in the garden
Than anywhere else on earth.

"God's Garden"—Dorothy Frances Gurney (1858–1932)

In the beginning, God created a garden, a beautiful garden to be both the home and place of sanctuary for all
humanity. Since the beginning of time, the garden has been
central to the human search for spiritual fulfillment and
the discovery of inner peace and contentment. Gardens
have long been associated with the human emotions of
tranquility, spirituality, and solace, allowing for a deep
sense of introspection. It is frequently in a garden setting
that one may connect with one's own soul and experience
the presence of a divine power through acts of prayer,
meditation, or contemplation. In a pleasant garden setting,
one tends to discover a sense of personal sanctuary, feels

drawn to nature, and becomes acutely aware of something far greater than self.

Leonard Sweet, in his groundbreaking treatise, *The Ten Commandments of Soulistic Health: Architecture for the Postmodern Reformation*, identifies as Commandment Number 4, "Thou shalt get the church out-of-doors." Sweet uniquely elaborates:

> Postmoderns will want to honor the world's oldest profession—and will celebrate the ministers of gardening in their midst. The church of the future will have extensive gardens—land gardens, water gardens and sky gardens (whether the spiritual or physical variety). There will be multitudes of sky-oriented spaces and places—shady nooks, basking places, star-viewing perches. The church will bring earth and sky together through upward gestures like obelisks, statues, trees, enabling the spirit to move upward and onward.[2]

Thomas Moore, in his delightfully encouraging work, *The Re-Enchantment of Everyday Life*, also expresses such a need in a very soulful way: "We may have to learn again the mystery of the garden; how its external characteristics model the heart itself, and how the soul is a garden enclosed, our own personal paradise where we can be refreshed and restored."[3]

Gardens have long been associated with the human emotions of peace, solace, and spirituality, allowing for a deep sense of introspection. In a garden setting, we tend to discover a sense of personal sanctuary. Likewise, we are often made acutely aware of some thing, some power, greater than ourselves.

The simple act of spending quality time in a peaceful, well-designed garden allows the user to block out negative distractions and focus on the positive acts of prayer, contemplation, or meditation, thereby enhancing one's spiritual growth and development. Within the confines of a liturgical/prayer garden, it becomes possible to experience a dynamic regeneration of the spirit as one is distanced from the preoccupations and demands of living in an often chaotic, confused, and demanding world. One of the great benefits of a soulful garden experience is the stripping away of chaos and disorder to discover the basic fundamental joys of peace and contentment. As I noted in one of my earlier works:

> Spending time in the garden, either working with my hands or simply relaxing, has been a cherished time when my mind is cleared, little or no distractions are present, and I am able to hear God's voice speaking to my soul. . . . In a sanctuary garden one can find not only peace and solitude, but a more important, more exciting sense of re-enchantment for the soul.[4]

Soul work is vitally important to any religious tradition and practice. Providing appropriate and comfortable venues for people to draw closer to the Creator is much like offering a healing balm that refreshes and facilitates the much-needed human experience of re-enchantment of the soul.

Participation in outdoor worship activities certainly enhances our experience of God as the divine Creator of the majestic beauty that surrounds us. Thomas Moore adds to this concept by noting: "In a garden the soul finds its needed escape from life and entry into a space where eternity is more evident than time and where ritual arrangement of life is more important than the business of surviving and making progress."[5]

A garden setting is an established aid to the human healing process by creating an environment that is conducive to relaxation, contemplation, and stress reduction. Viewing nature, especially in a calm, serene garden setting, facilitates the post-operative healing process.[6] As a person relaxes, meditates, participates in outdoor prayer and worship events, and is able to reduce the stress levels present, inner or spiritual healing may also begin to influence physical healing. "To be psychologically healthy, human beings need to experience their natural setting—the setting we were designed for, which is a garden."[7]

Prayer gardens and other sacred, natural spaces may serve as comfortable places of sanctuary to accommodate the diverse rites, rituals, and practices of our personal spiritual disciplines. In addition, by designing and conducting corporate worship liturgies in an outdoor setting, it is possible to facilitate a deeper appreciation for the grandeur and beauty of God's creation. Sacred space, in concert with ritual, is truly a fundamental component of a dynamic faith experience.

In an outdoor worship setting, the participant discovers in quite dramatic and imaginative ways that God is unable to be contained within the walls of a building. For many, partaking in the liturgy of worship within a garden setting may provide a new and unique gateway to a more active and dynamic religious experience.

BIBLICAL PRECEDENTS

The best place to find God is in a garden.
You can dig for him there.

George Bernard Shaw (1856–1950)

In virtually every major religious tradition, one can dig a bit and discover that the image of the garden has played a key role in expressing and illustrating the spiritual truths inherent in its own unique core teachings. Not only does the garden function as the locus of a sacred creation account but it also serves in many faith traditions as the final gathering vessel or resting place at the end of one's life as we understand it. As such, our beginnings and our endings seem to take place in a garden setting. Therefore, creating sacred outdoor prayer and worship space acknowledges the truth that religious buildings are not the only vessels where viable spiritual communication may be accomplished.

While numerous references to gardens are found

throughout the scriptures, the following presents a limited selection focusing on those passages dealing with worship in one context or another. The images and metaphors discovered in these passages serve to illustrate and often clarify many of the basic teachings of our Christian faith. Most scripture references and citations are taken from *The Message: The Bible in Contemporary Language*, by Eugene Peterson as the author freely employs the image of the garden in his groundbreaking paraphrase of sacred scripture.

Genesis 2 speaks of the garden that God plants in Eden. In this location, God provides trees of all sorts—for beauty and from which humans may eat. God simply asks that the garden be well kept by his human creations. Other than refraining from eating the fruit from the Tree-of-Knowledge-of-Good-and-Evil, few restrictions had been placed upon the garden's residents.

Hence, it all began in what must have been a beautiful garden: a garden setting created by God. Here, in this earthly paradise, God created man, and later woman, with the desire that they blossom and flower, while keeping the garden in order. The garden paradise was succulent with foods to eat. In this pristine setting of home and sanctuary, man and woman could live abundantly and eternally, needing only to obey God's commands and so worship their divine Creator.

With the genesis of life taking place in a garden, God's human creation continued to explore the image of the garden—or any outdoor holy space—as a place of holy and divine worship. Moses, on Mount Sinai, meets God and receives the Ten Commandments. Mount Sinai is enveloped in smoke, and God's voice warns Moses to respect the holy mountain. Here, in this dramatic and powerful setting, God reveals himself and delivers his laws for all to observe.

Much of the story of Noah takes place in the out-of-doors. In concluding the landing narrative (Genesis 8:20-

21), the reader discovers that Noah, after reaching dry land, builds an altar for the worship of God. Certainly, Noah, in his offering of sacrifices upon the altar, rejoices that the sweet-smelling fragrances are pleasing to God.

In Genesis 21:31-33, we find that Abraham dug a well and named the place Beersheba or "Oath-Well." Following this act, Abraham plants a tamarisk tree and worships God at this place of thanksgiving.

Altars of sacrifice, altars of sharing, sacred altars of thanksgiving are integral components of the worship of God from the earliest of times.

Exodus 3:1-12 recounts the dramatic story of Moses and the burning bush. It was on the mountain of God (Horeb) that an angel of the Lord came to Moses appearing in flames of fire blazing from a bush. In his bewilderment, Moses questioned what was happening, and it was at that point that Moses hears God's voice instructing him to remove his sandals for he is standing on holy ground.

After God notifies Moses that he is to shepherd his people out of the land of Egypt and guide them to a land flowing with milk and honey, a land of refuge and sanctuary for God's people, Moses is put on notice that he will return to that very same spot and worship God. Here, then, is a holy and sacred spot on a mountainside reserved for and dedicated to the worship of God.

The garden as vessel of our human endings is reinforced in 2 Kings 21:25 where Amon is buried in "the Garden of Uzza." Likewise, when Manasseh died, his remains were interred in the palace garden (2 Chronicles 33:20). Our "endings" often find rest in a garden setting that serves as a sacred memorial place of remembrance. In fact, a revealing New Testament passage (1 Corinthians 15:35) vibrantly compares the "resurrection body" to the planting of a dead seed that becomes a flourishing plant. Much like the seed that emerges into a plant, the resurrection body that comes from it will also be dramatically different.

Much of the imagery depicted in the Song of Solomon

illustrates the importance of the garden as a place of worship; this garden being both sacred and adored, a place of refreshment and renewal. In several instances, one discovers in this poetic discourse that the senses are dramatically heightened when experiencing the pleasures of the garden. Yes, the garden becomes a place of praise and worship.

Joel 3:18 describes beautiful rivers flowing everywhere in Judah, along with "a fountain pouring out of God's Sanctuary, watering all the parks and gardens!" Gardens, in this passage, become sacred and holy because the divine waters flowing from heaven nourishes them, giving them the gift of life and beauty.

Throughout the writings of the Old Testament, God is often portrayed as the "Master Gardener," the One who creates and nurtures the garden for human beings.[8] The metaphor of God as "Master Gardener" is truly a very rich and comforting image—God as the Creator and Sustainer of life in its many and diverse forms.

The celebration of Baptism begins in an outdoor setting (Matthew 3:13-17; Mark 1:9-11). Jesus approaches John at the Jordan River and seeks water baptism. Although John at first objects, he finally consents to Jesus' request, making this river a sacred and holy vessel for the worship of God. Could there be a more fitting setting for the conduct of baptism as a means of welcome into the kingdom of God?

The transfiguration of Jesus takes place on a mountainside (Matthew 17:1-9; Mark 9:2-9; Luke 9:28-36). Peter, James, and John are with Jesus as his glory is revealed in a most dramatic and empowering way. Here, in this outdoor setting, in a vision of holiness, Moses and Elijah are seen with Jesus and the voice of God reveals Jesus to be his beloved Son. Interrupting the conversation between Jesus, Moses, and Elijah, Peter suggests that this is indeed a great moment and three altars or memorials be constructed in their honor. Even though Jesus dismisses this notion, it is clear to see that the setting has divine qualities: qualities conducive to praise and worship.

Jesus frequently spends time in a garden for much-needed periods of solitude or spiritual renewal. It is in the garden that Jesus often finds rest and refreshment for body, mind, and soul. Matthew writes in his gospel narrative (26:36): "Then Jesus went with them to a garden called Gethsemane and told his disciples, 'Stay here while I go over there and pray.' " The garden, for many, has become that sacred place where one's mind is cleared from the distractions of life and prayer, meditation, and contemplation are certainly facilitated.

Before Jesus is taken prisoner, he retreats, along with his disciples, crossing over the brook Kidron to a garden. Judas, knowing that Jesus often sought refuge in this particular garden, leads the Roman soldiers to this place of sanctuary where the soldiers and high priests come and arrest Jesus.

Jesus' body is removed to a garden near the site where he was crucified (John 19:39). Scripture tells us that a previously unused tomb was located in this garden and Jesus' body was placed here for anointing and burial following the day of Sabbath preparation. Cemeteries are often regarded as memorial gardens and typically function as a sacred and revered place of remembrance.

In the third post-resurrection appearance of Jesus (John 21:1-14), we find Jesus sharing a breakfast of bread and grilled fish with seven of his disciples. Perhaps more a passage focusing on fellowship, it does, however, lend itself to the garden worship setting. Here, around a campfire, the disciples finally realize it is Jesus inviting them to share a meal. There is no doubt that the disciples are in awe of what is happening to them at this moment, and their hearts are surely filled with praise and thanksgiving.

A meaningful New Testament passage, which also employs the garden as a metaphor, is uniquely evidenced in the Letter of James. In this brief passage, James is offering instruction for living a faithful Christian life and suggests: "So throw all spoiled virtue and cancerous evil in the garbage. In simple humility, let our gardener, God, land-scape you with the Word, making a salvation-garden of your life" (James 1:20-21 *THE MESSAGE*). Because of the implied sacredness of gardens in the writings of the Christian faith, as one disposes of that which is evil and spoiled, life becomes a garden landscaped by God's goodness. Worship, then, becomes much more meaningful and pleasing to God the Creator.

Worship, in its many diverse forms and functions, may certainly take place in a garden or most anywhere in the out-of-doors. In today's world, gathering with others in a garden environment provides not only a calming and refreshing setting but also a deeply memorable worship experience.

LITURGIES

The liturgies developed in this text are meant to provide a basic means of inspiration for the planning and conduct of vibrant and meaningful worship experiences in an outdoor environment, especially in a garden setting. Experience has shown that a sense of peace and contentment is easily attained in an intimate, comfortable garden setting, thereby allowing participants to focus on the liturgy and, therefore, be more receptive to the Spirit of God moving in surprising ways.

Christian fellowship will surely be heightened dramatically as people share in the visible drama of God's creation around them. Such alternative settings present worship in new and life-giving ways. In fact, liturgical experiences in the garden may also foster a deeper sense of community while, at the same time, facilitating the creation of a bridge between many different faith traditions. In a garden, the focus is principally on God as the One we worship, devoid of the many trappings of denominationalism and sectarianism, elements which may, at times, detract from true worship.

In essence, the materials presented are the primary or

keystone elements of the worship service. The liturgies herein are meant to give meaning to the overall service while highlighting the outdoor experience for those who journey in faith and share in the rituals of faith. While in certain instances the materials set forth constitute a complete worship service, others may need to be woven into a more complete worship liturgy.

There exists in the life of the church numerous opportunities to experience and participate in worship in an outdoor setting. From small-group gatherings designed for a particular purpose to the participation of an entire congregation, outdoor worship uniquely adds to the fellowship and intimacy of the faith experience. Some of the most memorable faith experiences occur outside the traditional church structure, a reminder that Christ is present at all times and in all places. In the garden setting, we are immersed in the knowledge that all creation is the work of God and, as such, all creation is to be regarded as sacred.

CELEBRATING
GOD'S CREATION

An outdoor setting—especially within the confines of a garden—is a most appropriate venue to worship God and experience the fellowship shared by companions on the journey of faith. The garden setting is especially conducive to those worship services that function to proclaim the creative powers of God.

THEME
God is both proclaimed and honored as Creator.

GREETING
Good morning! Welcome to our service of worship and celebration this morning. We gather this day to honor and proclaim God as Creator. In the fellowship of Christ Jesus and one another, surrounded by the beauty of this garden, we seek God's blessing for all of creation. In the dynamic act of creation, God makes, separates, gathers, blesses, sees, and rests. As we have done in times past, let us now worship God, our Creator.

CALL TO WORSHIP

We gather this day, in this garden, to express gratitude for
the dramatic beauty of God's creation.
**Through God's blessings all things were created in
heaven and on earth.**
The whole of creation describes God's glory.
**A tapestry of sight and sound that embraces us when we
open ourselves to God's presence.**
The Lord reigns, let the earth be glad.
**Let all of creation resound with truth and beauty to the
ends of the ages.**

GATHERING PRAYER (UNISON)

**Gracious God, creator of the heavens and the earth, we
marvel at the beauty of your works. In the beginning, you
formed all humanity from the dust of the ground and shared
with us the breath of life. You set us in a garden of paradise
and called us to be faithful stewards of your creation.**

**Yet, like Adam and Eve, we have hidden from you,
attempting to conceal our faults and failures. Not only
have we rebelled against you but we have also failed in
our responsibility as stewards, taking advantage of
resources and gifts you share with us.**

**Through this simple act of worship, O Creator, help us
each to reaffirm our commitment for the care of your holy
creation. Empower us for acts of stewardship and
renewal that your glory may be manifest in our acts of
service and compassion. In Jesus' name we pray. Amen.**

DAY ONE

Light, Dark and God's Spirit

Genesis 1:1-5 (THE MESSAGE)

A reading from Genesis, chapter 1, verses 1 through 5.
Hear now the creative word of God.

First this: God created the Heavens and Earth—all you

see, all you don't see. Earth was a soup of nothingness, a
bottomless emptiness, an inky blackness. God's Spirit
brooded like a bird above the watery abyss.
God spoke: "Light!"
And light appeared.
God saw that light was good
and separated light from dark.
God named the light Day,
he named the dark Night.
It was evening, it was morning—
Day One.

MEDITATION

Until God speaks, nothing exists but darkness and chaos.
With the voicing of God's Spirit across the abyss of darkness
and nothingness, the sweeping cycle of creation begins. The
inky blackness that was present is now divided, separated
into dark and light, night and day. Until God voices—think
sings—creation into being there exists nothing but a formless void, a void that is totally chaotic. Yet, even in such a
dark and foreboding state of nothingness, God is completely
in control of the events taking place. It is God's restless and
creative Spirit that begins to shape and mold a perfect universe. Darkness is now only a part of what exists.

As the divine architect of creation, God has a plan, a
design, a pattern for transforming chaos into cosmos in a
way that sings of the goodness and glory of God. The creation narrative becomes a hymn or symphony about God
our Creator.

Throughout the ages darkness has often been associated
with the rather unfamiliar, frightening situations we
encounter in life. In a mysterious yet comforting way, God
is always present to bring order into our lives, creating
wholeness out of chaos. Light and dark now sets the stage
for the ordering of the universe, the days we live by, and
the ebb and flow of seasons. Just as the Spirit of God was

hovering over the abyss of darkness at the onset of creation, the Spirit continues to hover over our lives to bring forth light to illuminate our path. That light is Jesus, the Son of God, our Creator.

UNISON PRAYER

God of all creation, the voice of your Spirit sings this cosmos into being. You set the earth spinning, and your presence established night and day. Lord, we are thankful that your Spirit continues to shed light on our lives that we may clearly see the way to journey in faith. Help us, Lord, to always feel the warmth of your presence, knowing that darkness, fear, and foreboding moments will be swept away by your Spirit. For your works of creation, we offer our thanks.

How joyous it is, O God, to be a part of this creation celebration. You bring the world into being and with the voicing of your Spirit creating light and dark, night and day, and declare it to be good. Amen.

DAY TWO

Water and Air

Genesis 1:6-8 (THE MESSAGE)

We continue to hear God's creative Word from Genesis, chapter 1, verses 6 through 8.

God spoke: "Sky! In the middle of the waters;
    separate water from water!"
God made sky.
He separated the water under sky
    from the water above sky.
And there it was:
    he named sky the Heavens;
It was evening, it was morning—
Day Two.

MEDITATION

From an inky expanse of nothingness, a formless void, God now acts to divide the waters into Heaven and Earth. God's creative Word speaks and the primordial waters are separated into a terrestrial ocean and a celestial ocean. The celestial ocean is much like a thick, dense fog that envelops the earth: a canopy that covers the planet.

By creation of an atmosphere such as this, the lighter parts of the waters that covered the earth's surface were raised up and now appear suspended in the visible heavens above. The atmosphere becomes the medium for light and life. Both darkness and water are now under control; chaos is diminishing, and the stage is set for life to begin. Another day and God deems it good.

When someone appears confused we may say "they are in a fog." Just as God purified the fog that surrounded the earth as a means of creating an atmosphere to sustain life, God's Spirit is able to vanquish the fog that impedes personal clarity and growth. With a renewed sense of clarity, new visions, hopes, and dreams are possible as God is fully capable of creating and re-creating, molding and reshaping, transforming confusion and chaos into a more ordered life.

UNISON PRAYER

O God, your creative sweep continues, and a distinction is made between Heaven and Earth. Your voicing of creation continues to bring order out of chaos. How thankful we are that good things can emerge from our chaotic moments. You sweep away confusion and bring blessings of clarity and hope. We gather to bless your creation and offer our chaotic and confused lives to your control. Amen.

DAY THREE
Land and Plants

Genesis 1:9-13 (THE MESSAGE)
A reading from Genesis chapter 1, verses 9 through 13.
Creation continues.
God spoke: "Separate!
   Water-beneath-Heaven, gather into one place;
Land, appear!"
   And there it was.
God named the land Earth.
   He named the pooled water Ocean.
God saw that it was good.
God spoke: "Earth, green up! Grow all varieties
   of seed-bearing plants,
Every sort of fruit-bearing tree."
   And there it was.
Earth produced green seed-bearing plants,
   all varieties,
And fruit-bearing trees of all sorts.
   God saw that it was good.
It was evening, it was morning—
Day Three.

MEDITATION

Having already separated the waters, God now voices
the terrestrial waters to move so that dry land under the fir-
mament becomes visible. The pooled water is named
Ocean. As soon as land emerges, God begins to fill Earth
with seed-bearing plants and fruit-bearing trees. Order continues to be established, and the stage for life begins to take
shape. Variety, complexity, and even basic forms of hierar-
chy are being established by the sweep of God's Spirit.

During this particular day, there are really two distinct
acts of creation taking place: the emergence of dry land
and the establishment of life-sustaining vegetation. The
earth has now changed from a whirling mass of dark water

to a planet with great oceans, continental landmasses, and life-sustaining vegetation. In both acts of creation, God reflects on what has been accomplished and again calls it good. In fact, on this day, God twice rejoiced that the work accomplished was good, thereby marking it as a very special occasion.

Water is life: the medium of birth and growth. Likewise, plants provide nutrition, shelter, clothing, and many of the basic necessities of life. In these two acts, God's plan and pattern is taking shape in ways we could never imagine possible. Our place in God's creation is being prepared and, oh, how good it is!

UNISON PRAYER

O God, through your creative Word we now have earth and oceans and life-sustaining plants. Your wonders are without ceasing. Your creation is now sustaining basic life forms. You have made the plants and trees and grasses to grow. They sprout up and flourish in mysterious ways. Sustain us also, Lord, and allow us to grow and be life-sustaining elements of your creation. Help us also to be divine stewards of your earth and all its bounty. And, as we grow and mature in faith, look upon us and reaffirm our goodness. Amen.

DAY FOUR

Sun, Moon and Stars

Genesis 1:14-19 (THE MESSAGE)

From Genesis, chapter one, verses 14 through 19, God creates the Sun, Moon, and Stars above.

God spoke: "Lights! Come out!
Shine in Heaven's sky!
Separate Day from Night.
Mark seasons and days and years,
Lights in Heaven's sky to give light to Earth."

And there it was.
God made two big lights, the larger
    to take charge of Day.
The smaller to be in charge of Night;
    and he made the stars.
God placed them in the heavenly sky
    to light up Earth
And oversee Day and Night,
    to separate light and dark.
God saw that it was good.
It was evening, it was morning—
Day Four.

MEDITATION

Lights appear and shine, giving light to earth and marking the days and seasons of time. The sun, moon, and stars are unveiled this day in all their majestic glory. They are set ablaze in the heavens above to light up the earth, to separate night and day, to order the seasons. In essence, this light is a continuing part of the creation process as we witness light exposing the earth on day two; light aids in drying up the land on day three; and on the fourth day, it ignites in the heavens above.

Sun, moon, and stars serve as the great luminaries to the world of God's creation as they regulate and order the progress and divisions of time through their motions and movement. The sun marks the day, the moon marks the months, and the stars mark the seasons.

How majestic it is that God not only created the sun, moon, and stars to illuminate our days and nights but also to bring order to the cosmos. God's creative powers continue to establish and reestablish the earth as a more inhabitable place of sanctuary.

As the moon and stars receive their light from the sun in order to illuminate the darkness, so also the Church receives its light from Christ to reflect on those who live in the darkness of a sin-filled world. Faithful disciples of God's creation are, in turn, designed and called to reflect the light of Christ Jesus to others. Day four comes to an end, and God calls it good.

UNISON PRAYER

Holy, holy, holy are you the God of never-ending creation. On this day, we have witnessed the placement of sun, moon, and stars in the heavens above. A sense of order is now emerging, bringing light and dark, motion and movement, seasons and sanctuary. Light bursts forth to break away the bonds of darkness and the heavens above are ignited in divine glory.

Lord, may we your faithful witnesses, also set ablaze this earth with the light of your Son, Christ Jesus. As elements of your creation, help us to be the lampstands that illuminate the way of truth and hope in a broken world. Let each of us reflect the presence of the One who is Light. Amen.

DAY FIVE

Creatures of the Sea and Sky

Genesis 1:20-23 (THE MESSAGE)

Hear how God's creation continues and life begins with these words from the first chapter of Genesis, verses 20 through 23.

God spoke: "Swarm, Ocean, with fish and all sea life!
    Birds, fly through the sky over Earth!"
God created huge whales,
    all the swarm of life in the waters,
And every kind of species of flying birds.
    God saw that it was good.
God blessed them: "Prosper! Reproduce! Fill Ocean!
    Birds, reproduce on Earth!"
It was evening, it was morning—
Day Five.

MEDITATION

On the fifth day of the creation event, God forms the creatures of the seas and skies. The waters and the air is now teeming and swarming with life. Not only are the seas and air abundant with God-given life but God also calls these animals to prosper and reproduce. The earth is now alive with living creatures, and God blesses their presence. Actually, this is the first time that God blesses, and it is a most divine act of God's creation of living species. Sharing a word of blessing with the animals, God performs a powerful act of love, speaking to their very soul; the word of blessings is, "Prosper! Reproduce!"

Fish of the sea and birds of the air, each and every species all created by God. There is nothing evil in God's creation, and as part of God's creation event, human beings must consider a sense of responsibility to them. Are we not to honor, respect, and be good and faithful stewards of all of God's creation? When humanity comes to understand this all-important aspect of creation, we will truly begin to comprehend our similarities and learn to extend greater respect for the animal kingdom. Are they not our kindred souls having been created as we humans have been created, by the divine work of God?

This day and God's profound acts within it set the stage for the creation of the human species in day six.

UNISON PRAYER

Saint Francis is widely known as the patron Saint of animals. In our gathering today, I invite you to share in a reading of St. Francis of Assisi's Prayer for Animals.

God Our Heavenly Father,
You created the world
to serve humanity's needs
and to lead them to You.
By our own fault
we have lost the beautiful relationship

which we once had with all your creation.
Help us to see
that by restoring our relationship with You
we will also restore it
with all Your creation.
Give us the grace
to see all animals as gifts from You
and to treat them with respect
for they are Your creation.
We pray for all animals
who are suffering as a result of our neglect.
May the order You originally established
be once again restored to the whole world
through the intercession of the Glorious Virgin Mary,
the prayers of Saint Francis
and the merits of Your Son,
Our Lord Jesus Christ
Who lives and reigns with You
now and forever. Amen.

DAY SIX

Animals and Humans

Genesis 1:24-31 (THE MESSAGE)

God creates animals and human beings in this account
from the first chapter of Genesis, verses 24 through 31.

God spoke: Earth, generate life! Every sort and kind:
    cattle and reptiles and wild animals—all kinds."
And there it was:
    wild animals of every kind,
Cattle of all kinds, every sort of reptile and bug.
    God saw that it was good.
God spoke: "Let us make human beings in our image,
    make them
    reflecting our nature
So they can be responsible for the fish in the sea,
    the birds of the air, the cattle,

And, yes, Earth itself,
and every animal that moves on the face of the Earth."
God created human beings;
he created them godlike,
Reflecting God's nature.
He created them male and female.
God blessed them:
"Prosper! Reproduce! Fill Earth! Take charge!
Be responsible for the fish in the sea and birds in the air,
for every living thing that moves on the face of
Earth."
Then God said, "I've given you
every sort of seed-bearing plant on Earth
And every kind of fruit-bearing tree,
given them to you for food.
To all animals and all birds,
everything that moves and breathes,
I give whatever grows out of the ground for food."
And there it was.
God looked over everything he had made;
it was good, so very good!
It was evening, it was morning—
Day Six.

MEDITATION

During day six, a further advance is evidenced as God
creates the terrestrial species of animals, which are
included in three broad classes: (1) cattle, (2) reptiles, and
(3) wild animals of the earth. There appears to be general
consensus that the word "cattle" refers to domesticated
quadrupeds: all sorts of domesticated land animals. Reptiles, as a broader life-form, would then include those
smaller animals that creep, crawled, walked, or slid close
to the earth. Wild animals are then considered in general
terms as the untamed creatures of earth.

The ultimate stage of the creation event is now being

reached. God now says, "Let us make human beings in our image, make them reflecting our nature" (Genesis 1:26). While God is not physical or material, human beings were created in the likeness of God, in that humans have an intellect, emotion, and a will. Essentially then, human beings were created to be spiritually, intellectually, and morally like God. In the Fall, however, human being's nature was damaged and forever tarnished by sin. Even so, human beings are God's special creation.

God supplied all the food that was necessary for life: seed-bearing plants and fruit-bearing trees. "Whatever grows out of the ground," said God "I give for food."

In the concluding moments of this day, God declared the creation to be good. Six times God has declared the works of creation to be good; however, now that the final stage of creation has been reached and completed, God pronounces it "so very good!" All the significant components of God's plan were now in place and were functioning in harmony as God intended.

Because of God's divine creation event, we must never cease to honor and uphold God's divine acts. All of creation seems to have been made for our benefit and enjoyment, that we would always see God's glory in every other living soul and work of creation so that we might praise our Creator and rest in God's abundance, resting, as God rested, on the seventh day.

UNISON PRAYER

O Lord, how majestic is your name throughout all of creation. Your works have been brought to light and given life. With a sweep of your hand and a murmur from your voice the animals and humanity have taken their place in your creation. We are so thankful, Lord, for the act of being created in the image of your spirit, emotion, and intellect. Help us, Lord, to honor and respect all that you have made. We thank you, Creator, that you paused at the completion of every day and declared it good. Teach us, now to experience Sabbath rest. Amen.

DAY SEVEN

Sabbath Rest

Genesis 2:1-3 (THE MESSAGE)

The sweeping act of creation is complete, and we hear God taking Sabbath rest. A reading from the Second chapter of Genesis, verses 1 through 3.

Heaven and Earth were finished,
down to the last detail.
By the seventh day
God had finished his work.
On the seventh day
he rested from all his work.
God blessed the seventh day.
He made it a Holy Day.
Because on that day he rested from his work,
all the creating God had done.

MEDITATION

Down to the last minute detail, creation is completed, and God has finished the work at hand. Now God rests. God blessed the seventh day and sanctified it and set it apart. In this immensely important act, God is setting the time pattern for the remainder of the future.

This is the day the Lord has made, and we are instructed to rest and enjoy all that the Sabbath has in store for us. On this seventh day, God rested, not because God was tired, but rather because it was a cessation from work. It goes without saying that humans put a lot of labor into some creative undertaking, and even though one may not be bodily tired, it is soothing to just sit back and relax and reflect on the creative act experienced. In truth, such Sabbath rest and reflection is both soothing and refreshing.

Yes, God rested, blessed the seventh day, and made it a Holy day! "Yes, because in six days GOD made the Heavens and the Earth and on the seventh day he stopped and took a long, deep breath" (Exodus 31:17 (THE MESSAGE)).

If we work on the Sabbath, then we are focused on human, earthly work and not on God's will for our lives. If, on the other hand, we seek God's will and heed God's instruction, then we will continually rest in the embrace of God's love and grace.

It is quite clear in examining these passages describing God's creation event, that two types of Sabbaths are being proclaimed: a Sabbath made holy to the Lord our God (a Sabbath on which one is instructed to cease worldly activity and spend time worshiping, honoring, and praising God) and a Sabbath time of rest and renewal for all of God's creation, that all may be nurtured and refreshed.

UNISON PRAYER

Lord, God of Creation, your Spirit's voice called this Earth and all its fullness into being. A voice that swept over the waters of an abyss black with nothingness and formed life in all of its variety: Earth and Heaven, oceans and seas, plants and animals, and human life. And when this work was completed, you rested. Sabbath rest is so important for you and for us. We thank you, Creator, for the movement of your Spirit, your creating fingertips as they point us to behold the goodness around us, your renewal of all that is good. Fill our hearts with the joys we've experienced this day, and send us forth from this garden seeking truth and beauty, peace and justice, love and compassion for the totality of your creation. Amen.

From the second chapter of Genesis, verse 4, we conclude our service of celebration of God's creation with these words:

This is the story of how it all started,
   of Heaven and Earth when they were created.

BENEDICTION

As we leave this Garden of God's creation,
   may our praise and worship continue;
May we always seek truth and beauty,
   joy and unity, and,
May we also go in peace,
   as faithful stewards of God's creation. Amen.

BAPTISM OF THE LORD

Jesus' baptism in the Jordan both publicly and quite dramatically identifies Jesus as the Christ, the Chosen One of God. His baptism by John also sets the stage for Jesus' ministry as the long-awaited Messiah, whose coming is proclaimed by the prophet Isaiah (42:1-19). It is through the act of baptism of Jesus that we come to trust in the saving grace of Jesus Christ as Lord and Savior.

THEME

Christ's divine glory is dramatically revealed in his baptism at the Jordan River.

GREETING

God's Spirit is among us, calling us to journey in faith. Like a dove, God's Spirit descends on us as we gather in praise and prayer. As we remember the baptism of Jesus, our Lord, let us also remember our own baptism and be thankful.

CALL TO WORSHIP (RESPONSIVELY)

This is a day of joyous new beginnings.

We remember the baptism of Jesus, the beginning of his earthly ministry.

From the moment of his baptism by John,

and the gift of God's Spirit like a dove,

Jesus understood his call from God.

Through this ritual of remembrance may we also be reminded that

God calls each of us to share in the cleansing waters of God's love.

Open our hearts and spirits to your call, Lord, that we may journey in faith proclaiming good news to all.

GATHERING PRAYER (UNISON)

O God, your voice hovers over the waters of creation and calls us into a journey of new beginnings. You speak this day, Lord, and may we hear the voice that Jesus heard at his baptism in the Jordan, saying, "You are my child, chosen and marked by my love, pride of my life."

Open the heavens, Lord, and descend upon us like a gentle dove that we, too, may stand in the waters with Jesus, cleansed and marked by your love. Free us then to be your disciples. Amen.

SCRIPTURE READING
LUKE 3:15-17, 21-22 *(THE MESSAGE)*

The interest of the people by now was building. They were all beginning to wonder, "Could this John be the Messiah?"

But John intervened: "I'm baptizing you here in the river. The main character in this drama, to whom I'm a mere stagehand, will ignite the kingdom life, a fire, the Holy Spirit within you, changing you from the inside out.

He's going to clean house—make a clean sweep of your lives. He'll place everything true in its proper place before God; everything false he'll put out with the trash to be burned."

After all the people were baptized, Jesus was baptized. As he was praying, the sky opened up and the Holy Spirit, like a dove descending, came down on him. And along with the Spirit, a voice: "You are my Son, chosen and marked by my love, pride of my life."

MEDITATION
BY WATER AND THE SPIRIT

In today's gospel text, Jesus is baptized in the waters of a small river, the Jordan, which courses its way through a rocky valley near Jerusalem. Jesus joins his cousin, John, in these waters where John had been earlier baptizing multitudes and preparing the way for Christ.

Like our own baptism, Jesus' did not take long. And following the few moments of our own baptism, we spend a lifetime striving to learn what it means, how it has or will change our lives, and how God will act in our lives as we journey in faith.

All four gospels tell the story of Jesus' baptism, each in its own unique way, and yet, a wonderful core truth emerges from each account: Jesus is God's chosen and beloved Son. The four gospels also agree that this was a pivotal point in Christian history; Jesus' earthly ministry was ordained in this act of baptism by John. In fact, it is the event that inaugurates the proclamation of the good news of salvation for all of God's people. It was through this action that Jesus demonstrated what the saving love of God is all about.

God's answer to such selfless love comes as a voice from a cloud and the gift of the Holy Spirit in the form of a dove. What an incredible moment it must have been for Jesus to experience the limitless showering of God's grace and love in this most spectacular way. There is no doubt that Jesus was looking both forward and backward at that moment in time. He was looking backward, reviewing all the events in his life that led up to this water-washing moment and looking forward to the journey that lies ahead, all the opportunities for mission and ministry with which he has been charged.

Come, come with me to the Jordan River to that wilderness setting where John is preaching repentance and baptizing away the sins of those who choose to wade in the water. Of course, there was no reason that Jesus needed to be baptized; unblemished, undefiled, and totally pure, Jesus did what he did to fulfill all righteousness. In many ways, it can be said that Jesus waded in the waters of the Jordan with John to give us the example of his oneness with us and to demonstrate in a most dramatic way what the saving love of God is like and what we might expect from it. Also, it was in that moment of baptism that Jesus received God's precious outpouring of the Holy Spirit.

It was in that gift of the Holy Spirit that Jesus was empowered to go forward in public ministry teaching, forgiving and healing. And in much the same way, our ministry begins in the same place as did that of Christ Jesus and we, too, are called to go forward in mission and in ministry, caring for others, empowering them, loving them, and helping to heal their hurts and sorrows.

Today we remember how Jesus was baptized in the Jordan and how we have followed our Savior through those same waters, born again into the work of the church and into the greater community of believers. As we journey through life, as we journey through faith, we are reminded of the transforming power of Jesus Christ, made real and made visible at his baptism. In fact, the gospel writer states that the Holy Spirit, in baptism, "[will change you] from the inside out" (Luke 3:16-17 *THE MESSAGE*). May your lives be renewed over and over again at the precious font of God's redeeming love.

Whenever we remember our own baptism, we begin to contemplate how our identity is so closely intertwined with that of Jesus. Our own baptism joins us to Christ's death and resurrection and provides for us a new identity as children of a living and loving God. When we consciously take time to reflect on this sacred act, we begin to more fully experience the new beginnings and the fullness of life that God has in store for us.

CLOSING PRAYER

Gracious and loving God, we thank you for the waters of creation, the refreshing waters of life, and the renewing waters of baptism. For in these life-giving waters, we are buried with Christ in his death, share in his resurrection, and are reborn in the Holy Spirit. Help us, Lord, as those who have been baptized in your name, to hear your voice, and deliver the refreshing, renewing, living waters to others. Amen.

BENEDICTION

As we leave this garden of remembrance, may God's Spirit remain close. May we experience renewal and transformation and, like Jesus, be marked by God's precious love this day and always. Go in peace, sharing the love of Christ Jesus, our Savior. Amen.

BAPTISMAL SERVICE

Just as Jesus was baptized in the Jordan River, the garden now becomes a sacred and fitting venue for the conduct of this baptismal celebration. The intimacy provided in such a setting, along with the fellowship derived in a place of comfortable sanctuary, adds immensely to the impact and meaning of the service.

THEME
As the genesis of life began in a garden setting, new life commences at the font of God's grace and love.

GREETING
Besides being a sign of our belonging to God, the sacrament of Baptism is also a sign of our belonging to one another in a community of faith. We gather in community this day recognizing that baptism is an outward sign of an inward and spiritual blessing. Let us worship God our Creator.

CALL TO WORSHIP

Come to the waters of baptism; wash and be made clean in
spirit.

Baptize us with water and the heavens shall open up.

Come to the waters of baptism, and voice your praise for
God's love.

**Baptize us with water, and the Spirit of God shall
descend like a dove.**

May we who have been called through the waters of
baptism

live our lives at the font of God's love and grace.

GATHERING PRAYER (UNISON)

**God of all creation, you nourish us with living waters
and call us in one hope of your calling: one Lord, one
faith, one baptism. Through this Sacrament of your love
and grace, declare (*candidate's name*) to be a child of your
kingdom, a sheep of your flock that he/she may walk in
the newness of life, united with us, as instruments of
your righteousness. Today we gather in this garden to
share in your precious gift of baptism of (*candidate's
name*), and in so doing, we, along with you, proclaim
him/her a child of blessing, a child of promise. Amen.**

SCRIPTURE READING
MATTHEW 3:13-17 (*THE MESSAGE*)

Jesus then appeared, arriving at the Jordan River from
Galilee. He wanted John to baptize him. John objected,
"I'm the one who needs to be baptized, not *you!*"

But Jesus insisted. "Do it. God's work, putting things
right all these centuries, is coming together right now in
this baptism." So John did it.

The moment Jesus came up out of the baptismal waters,
the skies opened up and he saw God's Spirit—it looked
like a dove—descending and landing on him. And along

with the Spirit, a voice: "This is my Son, chosen and
marked by my love, delight of my life."

MEDITATION

Family members, friends, and all who share in this
momentous occasion, we have gathered this day to celebrate the gift of a precious new life offered by God. This
morning we share in the unique honor and responsibility
of participating in this Sacrament of Baptism. This celebration is truly meant to be a watershed moment in the life of
(*candidate's name*).

In the cleansing waters of baptism, we are symbolically
buried with Christ, and rising out of the waters, we share
in Christ's resurrection to eternal life. In much the same
way, (*candidate's name*) is today reborn for eternity
through this gift of water and the Spirit of a living and loving God.

Saturated in the waters of baptism, we enter into the
eternal fellowship of the communion of saints. What I
mean by this is that we share forever with all those who
have given over their lives to the care and love of God in
Jesus Christ by faith. In a truly comforting and reassuring
way, it includes all those who name themselves as followers of Jesus Christ: those who stand with us today, all those
who have gone on in glory before us, and those who will
follow in our footsteps.

When the earth was nothing but a dark, foreboding
abyss and the waters churned in unrelenting chaos, the
Spirit—the voice—of God moved over those waters and
brought order and life to the cosmos. In the ancient world,
water symbolized chaos and death. Yet, from these primordial waters, God creates light and dark; sun, moon and
stars; plants and animals; and, ultimately, the human
species, and declares these works to be good.

In the refreshing waters of baptism, we become part of
the household or family of God. We enter into a new life-

giving and life-sustaining relationship with Jesus Christ, the Savior of the world. Today, in this solemn act of baptism, we receive a host of new family members. And, for their lives becoming intertwined with ours, we say thanks be to God.

There are, in fact, several ways to become an integral part of a family. You may be born, adopted, or marry into a family and so establish a vital relationship with others. And today I tell you that baptism is not unlike a marriage ceremony by which you become a part of God's family. The Apostle Paul likened the waters of baptism to the waters of a womb, so in this baptism, (*candidate's name*) is born into the Christian life, surrounded by a family of God's creation.

Not only do these waters of baptism link us with Christ's death and resurrection but they also symbolize the cleansing of human sin and the purification of our souls. Baptism is indeed a beautiful expression of God's redeeming love that is freely and unconditionally given to us.

So, dear (*candidate's name*), love is truly what baptism is all about. It is God's love poured out for you and promised to you in many ways and claimed on your behalf by those of us who love you. God's love for you will always be there to watch over you, meet your needs, encourage you, and guide you as you journey in faith as one of the baptized, born anew in the faithful embrace of our Savior.

Living into our baptisms is certainly hard work. Alone, I can assure you, we are not capable of doing it, but with God's help, all things are possible. And, because all things are possible with and through God, we can joyously proclaim with great conviction, "I will live into my baptism with God's help."

(*Candidate's name*), may the God of love embrace you, always be with you, and may you seek to reflect that love in the world today. Go now in peace, and may the grace of Jesus Christ, the love of God, and the fellowship of the Holy Spirit be with you now and always. Amen.

INVITATION TO BAPTISM

Brothers and sisters in Christ,
through the Sacrament of Baptism,
we are received into Christ's Holy Church
and given new life through water and the Spirit,
forever sharing in God's gift of salvation,
forever marked as a disciple of Jesus Christ.

THANKSGIVING OVER THE WATER

We thank you, God,
   for this life-sustaining gift of water.
At the beginning of Creation,
   when deep, dark waters churned in chaos,
   your Spirit moved over them
   and transformed darkness into light.
In the time of Noah,
   you vanquished evil in the waters of a flood,
   and gave the Earth a new beginning.
Through the turbulent waters of the Red Sea,
   you led your children out of bondage
   and into the land of hope and promise.
Saturated in the waters of new life,
   your Son received the baptism of John,
   was anointed by your Holy Spirit
   as the Messiah, the Christ,
   to lead us through his death and resurrection
   from slavery to sin into the realm of eternal life.
We thank you, God,
   for these cleansing waters of Baptism.
In them we are buried with Christ into his death
   and raised by your grace to new live.
Through these waters of salvation
   we are born anew in your Spirit.
By the moving of your Holy Spirit once again,
   please bless these waters,
   that those baptized in them today

will be cleansed from sin, be born anew,
and continue forever in the risen life of Christ Jesus.
By this baptism may (*candidate's name*) have a new identity in Christ.
To you, O God,
with Christ Jesus, and the Holy Spirit,
be all honor and glory,
now and for all time.
Amen.

BAPTISM WITH LAYING ON OF HANDS

Parents and sponsors are invited to gather at the font along with the candidate.
(*Candidate's name*) I baptize you in the name of the Father,
and of the Son, and of the Holy Spirit.

Following the baptismal ritual, others in attendance may be invited to the font. The pastor and the candidate's family will lay hands on the candidate's head, and others may connect in a similar fashion. At this point, the pastor may anoint the candidate's forehead with oil and say:

The Holy Spirit work within you,
that being born through water and the Spirit,
you will journey in faith as a disciple of Christ Jesus.
(*Candidate's name*), you are sealed in baptism by the Holy Spirit
and forever marked as a child of God.

PRAYER OF THANKSGIVING (UNISON)

God of gentleness and love,
you have shared with us the gift of this child (*or candidate's name*).
Let your blessings and strength rest upon this child.

Help each of us to see your image in this gift,
  that we may learn more of your love and grace.
Guide and protect (*candidate's name*) through
  all his/her days.
And, Lord, we pray that you will empower this
    congregation
  to be a positive influence in her/his life
  as we seek your guidance, your direction in
    all things.
This we pray in Jesus' precious name. Amen.

BENEDICTION

Go now with the blessing of God's creative Spirit,
  thankful for the gift of baptism,
    for in this water we have become one with Christ,
    and incorporated into Christ's body the church.
Go now in peace. **Amen.**

INFANT DEDICATION

THEME

Jesus welcomes the little children into his kingdom; therefore, we model his teaching in the rite of infant dedication.

GATHERING PRAYER (UNISON)

Gracious and loving God, you are always near to us.
For the gift of life embodied in this precious child,
  we praise you and offer our thanks.
May your Holy Spirit work within us
  as we offer and dedicate this child to you.
Help us, Lord, to be faithful to your calling
  as we journey in faith together, embraced by your love,
  guided by your Spirit, and taught by your Word. Amen.

SCRIPTURE READING
MARK 10:13-16 (*THE MESSAGE*)

The people brought little children to Jesus, hoping he
might touch them. The disciples shooed them off. But Jesus

was irate and let them know it: "Don't push these children away. Don't ever get between them and me. These children are the very center of life in the kingdom. Mark this: Unless you accept God's kingdom in the simplicity of a child, you'll never get in." Then, gathering up the children in his arms, he laid his hands of blessing on them.

MEDITATION
A LETTER OF DEDICATION

Dear (*child's name*),

I am writing this letter to you fully aware of the fact that you will not be able to read or truly understand it for many years to come. This morning, my letter is one of importance to you, and one of great promise to your parents, because your parents have brought you to this garden today to offer and dedicate your life to God.

In this sacred act of dedication, we gave thanks to God for the miracle of your birth and asked for God's help and guidance in bringing you up in a Christian environment. We especially prayed that you would learn about God's redeeming love as you grew and matured. And, as a congregation or community of faith, we promised to love, encourage, and support you as you come to know of Jesus and his place in your life.

I would like to remind you that, as a child of God, you are the recipient of God's precious and endearing love. In fact, God created the heavens and the earth with you in mind. Please know that God is with you at all times and in all places. God is there to rejoice in your accomplishments, to offer care and compassion in your times of need, and to offer solace and understanding in your times of sorrow.

God not only accepts you, (*child's name*), but God will also encourage you, love you, forgive you when your choices lead you away from God, and offer to you the gift of eternal life as you are restored to God's kingdom. As you grow in wisdom and responsibility, God will love you by giving you a choice, by calling you to accept Jesus, and to live as one who names himself/herself as a child of God, a follower of the kingdom.

Today, we mark your joining us upon the journey of faith, and we do so because our Lord tells us that such as you is the kingdom of God. When Jesus was on earth, he blessed the little children. This morning, I ask that this same Jesus will bless you and keep you, that he will make his face to shine upon you, and that he will share his love, grace, and peace, this day and forever. May you find the wonderful blessings of God resting upon you every day of your precious life.

Sincerely,

(*Pastor's name*)

The letter should be placed in an unsealed envelope and presented to the parents at the conclusion of the dedication ritual.

PARENT'S/SPONSOR'S PROFESSION OF FAITH

I ask you now, in the presence of God and this congregation, to answer the questions of faith by responding, "With God's help, we will."

Will you commit to raise this child in Christian love,
to pray for this child, and teach (*child's name*) to pray,
to seek God's Word as your guide in raising (*child's name*),
to live out the Gospel in your home, and
trust in God's promises made to you and this child?
If so, please answer, "With God's help, we will."
Will you partner with this congregation, seek out their help and guidance,
and lead this child to do the same?
If so, please answer, "With God's help, we will."

PRAYER OF DEDICATION

(*Parents to gather with pastor at the altar and pastor to hold infant.*)

Gracious and loving God, we rejoice in the gift of (*child's name*) whose parents offer this child in dedication to you this day. The members of this church now join with (*parent's names*) in giving thanks to you for this precious gift of new life. We pray, Lord, that you would watch over and bless (*child's name*) all the days of his/her life. We pray for strength and wisdom, as he/she grows in Christian faith. May this child's life bring glory and honor to you, a life which causes you to rejoice and be further blessed.

We pray for his/her parents, (*parent's names*), that they may nurture this child with love, faith, hope, and trust. We also pray for this your church and ask that you help us to function as effective guardians and spiritual mentors. We pray this in Jesus' name. Amen.

COMMENDATION AND WELCOME
Members of this community of faith,
I commend this dear child to your love and care
    and pray that you will nurture and guide this child
    by your love, and with your examples of faith,
    your teaching, and your dedication to serve God.

FAITH COMMUNITY RESPONSE (UNISON)
**We give you thanks, O God, for this precious gift of
    life,
    and we welcome him/her in Christian love.
By this act, we faithfully renew our covenant to be
    faithful disciples
    and to walk in the way of the Lord.
We affirm that we will maintain a life of unity,
    worship, and Christian service that will serve to
    nurture and support this child.
We promise that we will love, encourage, and support
    you
    in your Christian faith and life. Amen.**

The pastor is then encouraged to walk amongst the gathering introducing the child to the assembly, reminding all gathered of their promise to nurture this child in faith.

DISMISSAL WITH BLESSING
(AARONIC BLESSING FROM
NUMBERS 6:24-26)

(*Child's name*), the Lord bless you and keep you;
the Lord make his face to shine upon you,
   and be gracious to you;
the Lord lift up his countenance upon you,
   and give you peace. Amen.

CONGREGATIONAL REAFFIRMATION OF THE BAPTISMAL COVENANT

It is most appropriate to periodically renew and reaffirm the covenant promises made at our baptism. A gathering of the community of faith serves to magnify the meaning and intent of such a service of worship.

THEME
In reaffirming our baptismal covenant, we are reminded that God's Holy Spirit empowers us for Christian living.

GREETING
In our gathering this day, we renew our faith commitment and remember the sacred covenant made in our baptism. As a family of faith, a community of believers, we are bound together by one faith, one hope, and one baptism. Today we take water, bless it, and share it as a symbol of God's Holy Spirit raining down upon us. Let us worship God our Creator.

GATHERING PRAYER (UNISON)

Spirit of the living God, your loves falls fresh upon each of us as we gather to reaffirm the covenant made at our baptism. We have inherited this covenant from those who have gone on before us and have taught us the way of faith. Send your blessing of peace, love, and joy upon us this day as we renew our commitment to live out this covenant of faith. Empower us, by the gift and presence of your Holy Spirit, for living out our calling in your name. Amen.

SCRIPTURE READING
MATTHEW 3:13-17 (*THE MESSAGE*)

Jesus then appeared, arriving at the Jordan River from Galilee. He wanted John to baptize him. John objected, "I'm the one who needs to be baptized, not *you!*"

But Jesus insisted. "Do it. God's work, putting things right all these centuries, is coming together right now in this baptism." So John did it.

The moment Jesus came up out of the baptismal waters, the skies opened up and he saw God's Spirit—it looked like a dove—descending and landing on him. And along with the Spirit, a voice: "This is my Son, chosen and marked by my love, delight of my life."

MEDITATION
REMEMBER YOUR BAPTISM

When did you last remember your baptism? Many of you, no doubt, are thinking what a silly question. How could I ever be expected to remember my baptism, it was so long ago? It took place when I was just a baby, an infant, carried around in my mother's arms.

Of course, a great majority of us are unable to remember our baptism, if what we are thinking of is the actual day or the circumstances of the ritual. It is indeed difficult for many to even remember the name of the church or the pastor who officiated and who was present on that joyous day to witness the sharing in this sacrament.

It is fortunate that we have heard today from the gospel passage from Matthew, the passage in which he tells the story of Jesus' water baptism by John. Although brief, the passage from Matthew shares a very powerful message with the readers. As you hear these words, it is quite possible that you find yourself on tiptoes with expectation. In fact, it is hoped that, by hearing these words, you will be encouraged to live yourself into the gospel message: to live each and every day remembering the gift of your baptism.

In short, to remember your baptism is to dramatically recall what God has done for you through this sacrament. In baptism, God declared that you have been adopted into his greater family of faith. Though we were baptized once, we remain for the duration of our lives—and beyond—as one of the baptized: reborn by water and the Spirit. We are made into God's children, and formed into the family of God, by the grace of God's Holy Spirit.

Long ago, Jesus, in response to a question about being reborn, said to Nicodemus: "Unless a person submits to this original creation–the 'wind-hovering-over-the-water' creation, the invisible moving the visible, a baptism into a new life—it's not possible to enter God's kingdom" (John 3:5 THE MESSAGE). We are indeed God's people because God took the rather bold and daring initiative to reach out and embrace us in love and grace.

In the rite of baptism, the waters link us to Christ's death and resurrection. As one goes under the waters of baptism, it is not unlike dying and being reborn. In baptism, we believe that God's love is made real and visible so that we can better understand and accept that love. And joyously, that love comes to us through Jesus Christ who came to save us and give us new life.

In baptism, not only does God remind us of what he has done for us but God also illustrates how we are to live in response to his saving love. In fact, we are reminded in the baptismal liturgy also to surround the baptized with a community of love and forgiveness. To remember our baptism is to also dwell together in peace and unity, love and compassion, forgiveness and reconciliation. That is, we are challenged to live out the reality of God's presence in our lives celebrating the significance of our baptism and being "marked" as a disciple of Christ Jesus.

It should be emphasized that this is a renewal of our baptismal covenant, not a rebaptism. While baptism is a once-in-a-lifetime event, it should have a continuing impact throughout life. It is to remember that God's grace touches us with acceptance and blessing, unconditionally, perpetually, forever, always celebrating the significance of our baptism.

Remember your baptism and be thankful! Amen.

THANKSGIVING OVER THE WATER

In the beginning
the earth was a formless void,
and darkness covered the face of the deep.
At the very dawn of creation
God's Spirit swept across the waters
creating a fountain of divine holiness.
In the time of Noah
God cleansed the world with flooding waters
and placed a rainbow in the heavens above
as a sign of God's covenant with humanity.
The flood became a sign of the waters of baptism
that marked an end to sin
with an offer of new beginnings.
In time, God sent Jesus,
nurtured in the waters of a womb
as the Savior for all humanity.
In the waters of the Jordan River,
Jesus was baptized by John

and anointed by God's Spirit.
The power of water
  made known throughout the ages
  becomes a paradox
  both bringing forth life
  and sweeping life away.
And so, Christ Jesus calls his disciples
  to share in the baptism of his death and resurrection
  and to make disciples throughout God's creation.

Let us pray:
Creating God, let your Spirit flow over this gift of water;
  allow us to remember the grace declared in our own
    baptism
  as our sins were washed away.
  Remind us that by dying and rising with Christ
  we will one day share in Christ's final victory. Amen.

RITE OF REAFFIRMATION

*Water may sprinkled by dipping a small evergreen branch into
the water and gently shaking it in the direction of the gathering,
so as not to imply baptism by sprinkling. With each motion of
the dipped evergreen branch, the officiant will say:*
Remember your baptism in Christ Jesus and be thankful. Amen.

PRAYER OF THANKSGIVING (UNISON)

**God of creation, we voice our thanks for all that you
share with us. We thank you for creating and nurturing
this bountiful earth. Especially this day, we thank you
for gentle reminders of the covenant made at our baptism. Through our baptism, we are incorporated into
your mighty acts of salvation and made a part of the
body of Christ. May we strive to be holy and live out our
baptismal faith guided by your love, washed of our sins,
and embraced by your redeeming grace. In Jesus' name
we pray. Amen.**

BENEDICTION

May the God of creation and grace
Wash over your lives, and in so doing,
    fill your soul with hope,
    your heart with love,
    and your mind with Christ.
May the power of God's Spirit give you peace. Amen.

COMMUNION

In sharing the bread and wine of communion in unique ways and especially in an intimate garden setting, the experience should have a profound and lasting effect upon the participant. Although Jesus first shared the elements with his disciples in an upper room, a garden setting provides yet another uniquely intimate moment in which to experience the power of the risen Savior.

THEME

In the breaking of bread, and sharing of the cup, we are remembering the life, death, and resurrection of Jesus Christ. It is both a re-enactment and a divine remembrance of Jesus' final hours with his disciples.

INVITATION TO HOLY COMMUNION

Friends, this is a joyful feast to be shared by the people of God.

We are invited to the Lord's Table as those chosen, forgiven and reconciled.

Believe, come, and share in the goodness of God's abundant provision.

GATHERING PRAYER (UNISON)

Loving God, we praise you for the sheer beauty and splendor of your creation. We thank you for sustaining all that lives and grows. Your gifts are truly beyond measure.

Be among us now, Lord, as we share in this celebration of your never-ending love. Grant us strength as we journey through the seasons of life, always loved by your Son, Jesus the Christ, who gave himself on a cross of death that we might live.

Nourish and sustain each of us with your Holy Spirit that we may partake of this feast in truth and righteousness, ever mindful of Jesus' ultimate sacrifice to wash away the sins of the world. Bind us together, Lord, as a forgiven and reconciled people, forever sharing and caring in your precious name. Amen.

SCRIPTURE READING
1 CORINTHIANS 11:23-26 (*THE MESSAGE*)

Let me go over with you again exactly what goes on in the Lord's Supper and why it is so centrally important. I received my instructions from the Master himself and passed them on to you. The Master, Jesus, on the night of his betrayal, took bread. Having given thanks, he broke it and said,

This is my body, broken for you.
Do this to remember me.

After supper, he did the same thing with the cup:

This cup is my blood, my new covenant with you.
Each time you drink this cup, remember me.

What you must solemnly realize is that every time you eat this bread and every time you drink this cup, you reenact in your words and actions the death of the Master. You will be drawn back to this meal again and again until the Master returns. You must never let familiarity breed contempt.

EUCHARISTIC PRAYER

The Lord be with you.
And also with you.
Lift up your hearts.
We lift them up to the Lord of Creation.
Let us offer our praise and thanks to God.
It is right to give our praise and thanks.
It is right, always and everywhere to give thanks to God,
    the Creator of heaven and earth and of all its
abundance.
    You formed the sun and moon and stars above
        and embraced your creation with words that were
well-pleasing.
    You created oceans and dry land, mountains and valleys
        as home to plants and animals.
    You then formed us in your holy image, O God,
        and breathed life into each of us.
    You provided a Light in Christ Jesus to guide our way
        and bring us closer to you.
    When we turned away from you, Lord,
        your love was always present, arms always out-
stretched to welcome us.
    You have showed us how to walk in faith with dignity
and hope.
    You shared with us the promise of abundant and eternal
life,
        reminding us that sin and death are not the end.
    We are washed and made clean by the power of the
cross
        and the blood poured out in Jesus' death.
    We give you thanks, O God, for this holy meal,
        shared in remembrance of all that Christ gave for us.
    And so, Lord, bind us together as children of your
Creation,
        eager to follow in your way of truth and life,
        that we may always give you praise and thanks.

Through your abundant love given in the gift of Christ
Jesus,
    and shared in this Communion meal. Amen.

THE LORD'S PRAYER

And now, as forgiven and reconciled children of God, let
us pray together,
    Our Father, who art in heaven,
        hallowed be thy name; thy kingdom come,
        thy will be done, on earth as it is in heaven.
    Give us this day our daily bread;
    and forgive us our sins,
        as we forgive those who sin against us;
    and lead us not into temptation,
        but deliver us from evil.
    For thine is the kingdom and the power and the glory
forever. Amen.

BREAKING THE BREAD

Because we share in one loaf,
    we are reminded that though we are many,
    we are of one body and one in faith, hope, and love.
The bread that we break is a sharing in the body of
Christ.
    The cup containing the fruit of the vine
    is a sharing in the blood of our Savior.
    Thanks be to God.

SHARING THE BREAD AND CUP

Come. Come and share at the table of our Lord,
    open to all who believe in Christ Jesus as Lord and
Savior.
    Come, share in the Bread of Life and the Cup of
Salvation.

PRAYER OF THANKSGIVING (UNISON)

God of creation and new life,

with joy we have received this sacrament of bread and wine,

giving thanks for your Son, Jesus Christ, our hope and peace.

May we experience peace and unity

as we share in Christ's ministry of love and servanthood.

We thank you, God, for this holy mystery

in which you have given yourself to us.

And now, send us into the world

bound together in the strength and guidance of your Holy Spirit,

in the name of Christ Jesus our Lord. Amen.

DISMISSAL WITH BLESSING

Go now in peace, and may the

grace of our Lord Jesus Christ,

the love of God eternal,

and the communion of the Holy Spirit,

accompany you on your journey in faith. **Amen.**

WAY OF THE CROSS

The Way of the Cross or Stations of the Cross, and sometimes known as Via Dolorosa, or Way of Sorrows, refers to the depiction of the final hours (Passion) of Jesus the Christ. For many, it has been a moving way of participating in the suffering experienced by Christ as an integral alternative to traditional Good Friday services. Its essential inspiration evolved from a desire to re-create or imitate early Christian pilgrimages to the Holy Land as a means to visit the places (stations) of Christ's suffering from the moment of his arrest, to the time of condemnation to death, to the burial in a tomb.

Stations may be set along a pathway in the garden and may incorporate images or markers ranging from very simple (a Roman numeral attached to a post) to the installation of more elaborate and ornate art objects or other visuals. Either solution may be installed on a temporary or permanent basis.

While in most instances this form of devotion has typically declined in use, it is included as a means to make such a spiritual journey a rich and meaningful experience of prayer and devotion. The stations outlined in this liturgy are essentially adapted from *The United Methodist Book of Worship* (1992).

THEME

A spiritual pilgrimage of prayer and devotion as a vibrant means to experience Christ's Passion.

GREETING

Today, in this sacred garden, we embark on a solemn and meaningful journey: the Way of the Cross. Symbolically, we retrace Christ's steps from his time of prayer in the garden, to his arrest and condemnation, and ultimately to his crucifixion and burial. Our journey will include the reading of a passage of Scripture at each Station, a brief devotion, and a unison prayer. Come; come let us follow in the Way of our Lord.

FIRST STATION

Jesus Prays Alone

Luke 22:39-44 (THE MESSAGE)

Leaving there, he went, as he often did, to Mount Olives. The disciples followed him. When they arrived at the place, he said, "Pray that you don't give in to temptation."

He pulled away from them about a stone's throw, knelt down, and prayed, "Father, remove this cup from me. But please, not what I want. What do you want?" At once an angel from heaven was at his side, strengthening him. He prayed on all the harder. Sweat, wrung from him like drops of blood, poured off his face.

REFLECTION

In a garden, all alone, knowing that his death was imminent, Jesus prayed that this cup be taken from him, yet sacrificially, his desire was that God's will be done rather than a personal need or want be answered.

How often have we, in moments of pain and suffering, tragedy and tribulation, focused on self rather than the need for God's will to be done? Even in the awful experience of pain and sorrow, one needs to surrender to God's will as the best possible solution available. In the shadow times of life, when all seems dark and foreboding, spiritual growth is possible in the act of surrender.

A dear friend once offered sage advice when he said, "God will never place more burdens on you than you can bear." How true are these words.

UNISON PRAYER

Lord God, forgive my focus on self and for the times I seem to take you for granted. Help me to be mindful of my sinful nature and how I have hoped and prayed for my need to be met rather than your will be done. Have mercy on me, O Lord, a sinner. Help me to be more like Jesus as I follow in his way of truth and love. Amen.

SECOND STATION

Jesus Is Arrested

Matthew 26:47-56 (THE MESSAGE)

The words were barely out of his mouth when Judas (the one from the Twelve) showed up, and with him a gang from the high priests and religious leaders brandishing swords and clubs. The betrayer had worked out a sign with them: "The one I kiss, that's the one—seize him." He went straight to Jesus, greeted him, "How are you, Rabbi?" and kissed him.

Jesus said, "Friend, why this charade?"

Then they came on him—grabbed him and roughed him up. One of those with Jesus pulled his sword and, taking a swing at the Chief Priest's servant, cut off his ear.

Jesus said, "Put your sword back where it belongs. All who use swords are destroyed by swords. Don't you realize that I am able right now to call to my Father, and twelve companies–more, if I want them—of fighting angels would be here, battle-ready? But if I did that, how would the Scriptures come true that say this is the way it has to be?"

Then Jesus addressed the mob: "What is this—coming out after me with swords and clubs as if I were a dangerous criminal? Day after day I have been sitting in the Temple teaching, and you never so much as lifted a hand against me. You've done it this way to confirm and fulfill the prophetic writings."

Then all the disciples cut and ran.

REFLECTION

Betrayal comes from a trusted friend, and the hurt is deep and searing. One member of the inner circle turns traitor and points a condemning finger. Think of a time in your life when a dear friend has betrayed your trust, perhaps spreading some malicious gossip or somehow rallying against you in your time of need. Were you fortunate enough to have another ally come to your defense, or were you left standing all alone to bear the brunt of your detractors?

Think also of a time when you may have abandoned a friend in need, solely for your own gain, your own profit. How did you feel afterward, after the friendship was apparently destroyed? Repaying goodness with revenge or hurt or harm is certainly not the way of Jesus; nor is it the way of love and redemption.

UNISON PRAYER
Loving Lord, how often I have forsaken you: your teachings, your love, your friendship. How distraught

you must have felt. I have also abandoned family and friends in their time of need, never considering the hurt and betrayal they have felt. Forgive me, Lord, and enable me from this day on to be caring and compassionate in all my relationships. Amen.

THIRD STATION

Sanhedrin Tries Jesus

Mark 14:60-64 (THE MESSAGE)

In the middle of this, the Chief Priest stood up and asked Jesus, "What do you have to say to this accusation?" Jesus was silent. He said nothing.

The Chief Priest tried again, this time asking, "Are you the Messiah, the Son of the Blessed?"

Jesus said, "Yes, I am, and you'll see it yourself:

The Son of Man seated

At the right hand of the Mighty One,

Arriving on the clouds of heaven."

The Chief Priest lost his temper. Ripping his clothes, he yelled, "Did you hear that? After that do we need witnesses? You heard the blasphemy. Are you going to stand for it?"

They condemned him, one and all. The sentence: death.

REFLECTION

Imagine, if at all possible, how Jesus must have felt being tried and convicted by the religious authorities: the very people God entrusted with his sacred Word. Evidently stunned, Jesus never uttered a word in his own defense. Instead, out of God's precious gift of perfect love, God unconditionally forgave them for their actions, indicating that they would one day see him seated at the right hand of God, arriving there on clouds of glory.

When we are unjustly hurt by the words or actions of others, is our reaction to offer forgiveness and grace, or does revenge become our sole focus? God has so freely and unconditionally forgiven the sins of all humanity. Shouldn't we, according to Jesus' teachings, be able to forgive our neighbor?

UNISON PRAYER

Lord of love, there are no excuses whatsoever when I forsake you or when I abandon the needs of others. Teach me, Lord, to be both humble and forgiving. Show me how to love you completely, for then I too will be a gift to others. Amen.

FOURTH STATION

Pilate Tries Jesus

John 18:33-37 (THE MESSAGE)

Pilate went back into the palace and called for Jesus. He said, "Are you the 'King of the Jews'?"

Jesus answered, "Are you saying this on your own, or did others tell you this about me?"

Pilate said, "Do I look like a Jew? Your people and your high priests turned you over to me. What did you do?"

"My kingdom," said Jesus, "doesn't consist of what you see around you. If it did, my followers would fight so that I wouldn't be handed over to the Jews. But I'm not that kind of king, not the world's kind of king."

Then Pilate said, "So, are you a king or not?"

Jesus answered, "You tell me. Because I am King, I was born and entered the world so I could witness to the truth. Everyone who cares for truth, who has any feeling for truth, recognizes my voice."

REFLECTION

Jesus was innocent. He was not guilty of any crime, yet he was being tried by someone who neither knew nor cared about God's Holy Word. Imagine how the Son of God must have felt about being accused by people so unjust and as unforgiving as this foreign ruler. Imagine his distress at being hauled before an unbeliever to be judged for his conviction of sharing the message of truth.

Pause for a moment and think of the multitudes of people around the globe who are persecuted because of their beliefs. Are you strong enough in your faith and belief to face criticism or even persecution? If not, why not?

UNISON PRAYER

It is through your love, O God, that Christ Jesus was able to face those who despised him and to remain upright against the mighty winds of unrighteousness, even to death upon a cross.

O Lord, how often I have turned away when questioned about my faith or even dismissed my faith to others. Help me, Lord, to remain steadfast and true, as did your Son, when confronted by the enemy. This we pray in Jesus' name. Amen.

FIFTH STATION

Pilate Sentences Jesus

Mark 15:6-15 (THE MESSAGE)

It was a custom at the Feast to release a prisoner, anyone the people asked for. There was one prisoner called Barabbas, locked up with the insurrectionists who had committed murder during the uprising against Rome. As the crowd came up to present its petition for him to release a prisoner, Pilate anticipated them: "Do you want me to release the King of the Jews to you?" Pilate knew by this time that it was through sheer spite that the high priests had turned Jesus over to him.

But the high priests by then had worked up the crowd to ask for the release of Barabbas. Pilate came back, "So what do I do with this man you call King of the Jews?"

They yelled, "Nail him to a cross!"
Pilate objected, "But for what crime?"
But they yelled all the louder, "Nail him to a cross!"
Pilate gave the crowd what it wanted, set Barabbas free
and turned Jesus over for whipping and crucifixion.

REFLECTION

After being scourged and then crowned with thorns,
Jesus was taken before Pilate and unjustly condemned by
Pilate to die on a cross. Pilate had bowed to the demands
of the crowd who were poisoned by the religious authorities, urging them to call for his condemnation. Jesus
became an innocent victim of mob mentality, a victim led
to the slaughter.

Does mob mentality make things right? How often do
we hear of crowds pushing others into acting unjustly, perhaps even to the point of taking an innocent life? How
often, we might ask ourselves, does a chorus of voices
work together to break someone's spirit? Or life?

Remember, Jesus would have you forgive rather than
condemn.

Let us pray.

**God of amazing love and immeasurable forgiveness,
the brutal actions of a mob, in concert with an unright-
eous leader, led to the crucifixion of your Son, your only
Son. Hysteria, rather than peace, among people brought
about a death, an unjust death. Forgive me, Lord, for my
sins of condemnation to whatever degree they may be,
hurting others, and joining the chorus of negativity. Free
me, Lord, to bring glory to you in all my words and
actions. Help me to share the gift of truth and work for
justice. Amen.**

SIXTH STATION

Jesus Wears a Crown

John 19:1-5 (THE MESSAGE)

So Pilate took Jesus and had him whipped. The soldiers, having braided a crown from thorns, set it on his head, threw a purple robe over him, and approached him with, "Hail, King of the Jews!" Then they greeted him with slaps in the face.

Pilate went back out again and said to them, "I present him to you, but I want you to know that I do not find him guilty of any crime." Just then Jesus came out wearing the thorn crown and purple robe.

REFLECTION

Consider the pain and sheer anguish of having a sharp, penetrating crown of thorns pushed into your head. Picture, if you will, Jesus standing in front of the crowd, blood seeping down his face blurring his vision, unable to clearly see his tormentors. Standing there in total humiliation, Jesus exemplifies a bold faith that seemingly shouts out at his accusers, "Love one another as I have loved you. Even now, I love you all and care for you. Please, please care for one another."

UNISON PRAYER

Never have I thought about how painful it must have truly felt as you were tortured, beaten, and forced to wear a crown of thorns and mockingly paraded before the crowd in a purple robe. I doubt I could bear the hurt and humiliation, without screaming out in pain.

How I wish I could open my eyes and focus on you, Jesus, so that I might learn your perfect love and forgiving nature. Make it so, Lord Jesus, make it so. Amen.

SEVENTH STATION

Jesus Carries His Cross

John 19:17-18 (THE MESSAGE)

They took Jesus away. Carrying his cross, Jesus went out to the place called Skull Hill (the name in Hebrew is *Golgotha*), where they crucified him, and with him two others, one on each side, Jesus in the middle.

REFLECTION

Jesus had experienced the most horrendous journey in his life. It was a long, exhausting trek from Pilate's court to the place of crucifixion. Stumbling, falling, bleeding, wracked with pain, Jesus struggled to keep moving forward. And surely, in all those agonizing moments, Jesus was not thinking about himself but of us, the people of God's creation and how we might endure the trials and tribulations of keeping the faith.

Each of us has those crosses we must bear as we journey through life. How each of us bears these crosses can be made so much easier when we journey in complete faith and trust in a Savior who gave everything for us, a Savior whose love has set us free.

UNISON PRAYER

Help me, Lord, to endure the trials and tribulations that are a necessary part of life. Give me strength and courage to carry my cross and to carry it with patience. As I repent of my sins, may I know that you are always near to help carry the burden, share the load. May I never feel separated from your grace and grasp. Amen.

EIGHTH STATION

Simon Carries Jesus' Cross

Luke 23:26 (THE MESSAGE)

As they led him off, they made Simon, a man from Cyrene who happened to be coming in from the countryside, carry the cross behind Jesus.

REFLECTION

An unsuspecting wayfarer, Simon of Cyrene, is ordered to assist Jesus in the near unbearable burden he is carrying. A brief respite for Jesus, yet it is but for a brief moment in time. No doubt confused, even bewildered as to what is taking place, Simon offers to Jesus a great and lasting gift—his support.

"Must Jesus Bear the Cross Alone?" is an old hymn that asks a disturbing question of all who believe in the Son of God as Savior of the world. The sins of humankind played a significant role in placing this cross-carrying burden on Jesus and call us to remembrance of this tragic act. Jesus bore the cross for all humanity—couldn't we at least help, in some small way, to help carry this overwhelming burden?

Of course we can. Each act or word of kindness and forgiveness we offer; each act of praise and worship we experience; each and every offering of time, talent, or treasure is a generous gift which says to Jesus, "Lord Jesus, know that your journey was not made in vain. You are truly loved and deeply appreciated."

UNISON PRAYER

Gracious God, this journey has taught me that I, too, may have a cross to bear. Grant me the strength necessary to not only live for you but also to humbly carry those crosses I may be burdened with. Lord, share your grace, and may I always be aware of your comforting presence. Amen.

NINTH STATION

Jesus Speaks to the Women

Luke 23:27-31 (THE MESSAGE)

A huge crowd of people followed, along with women weeping and carrying on. At one point Jesus turned to the women and said, "Daughters of Jerusalem, don't cry for me. Cry for yourselves and for your children. The time is coming when they'll say, 'Lucky the woman who never conceived! Lucky the wombs that never gave birth! Lucky the breasts that never gave milk!' Then they'll start calling to the mountains, 'Fall down on us!' calling to the hills, 'Cover us up!' If people do these things to a live, green tree, can you imagine what they'll do with deadwood?"

REFLECTION

Distraught at seeing Jesus streaming with blood, weakened, and struggling to carry the burden of the cross, the women began weeping and carrying on. Isn't that a reaction that most of us display when we must face some dire tragedy in life? We weep and wail and carry on.

Everyone experiences grief at one time or another. This behavior, when carried out in a healthy way, leads to cleansing and understanding; it is essentially a vital component of the healing process. When one journeys in the way of faith, Christ is always there to offer a reaffirming word. At times, those words may seem sharp and cutting, "Do not weep for me, but weep for yourselves and your children." Jesus is perhaps telling us that there could be worse things in life that will come along and disturb our very being. Yet, with faith, we know that there is a Savior who offers consolation and compassion. Jesus encourages us to live, not just for self, but for him. And, it is in our living for Jesus that our lives are much like strong, green, and growing trees that will not be cast into the wood pile.

UNISON PRAYER

I have caused many, many sorrows in life, Lord, for others, for myself, and especially for you. Today, as I walk in your way of sorrows, I ask your forgiveness. Give me strength and understanding that I may avoid offending you and others. Yours is a love beyond measure, and I am indeed grateful for that gift. Help me to grow in your likeness. Amen.

TENTH STATION

Jesus is crucified.

Luke 23:33-34 (THE MESSAGE)

When they got to the place called Skull Hill, they crucified him, along with the criminals, one on his right, the other on his left.

Jesus prayed, "Father forgive them; they don't know what they're doing."

Dividing up his clothes, they threw dice for them.

REFLECTION

Knocked to the ground, forced upon a rough-hewn cross that further tore open the wounds from his whipping, Jesus is crucified. In that crucifixion moment, Jesus spread wide his arms, wrapped them around all of creation, and said, "See, this is how much I love you." Blow by blow, those deadly nails were driven through his flesh. The sound of iron driving iron must surely have echoed throughout the world as darkness enveloped creation.

In a redeeming act of love, Jesus asked God to forgive those who caused this terrible tragedy. His selfless act brought salvation to a hurting world. Piercing iron spikes held Jesus to that cross of terror. Suffering and experiencing great anguish, the cross was raised, and Jesus was left to die.

SILENT MEDITATION

ELEVENTH STATION

Criminals speak to Jesus

Luke 23:39-44 (THE MESSAGE)

One of the criminals hanging alongside cursed him: "Some Messiah you are! Save yourself! Save us!"

But the other one made him shut up: "Have you no fear of God? You're getting the same as him. We deserve this, but not him—he did nothing to deserve this."

Then he said, "Jesus, remember me when you enter your kingdom."

He said, "Don't worry, I will. Today you will join me in paradise."

REFLECTION

Hanging on that cross between two common criminals, Jesus is now being ridiculed by the very people he loved so dearly: people for whom Jesus extended healing, compassion, and great love. Forgetting his own pain and suffering, Jesus continues to offer compassion to the criminal who asked for forgiveness, promising him that he would later that day join Jesus in paradise.

Imagine a time of your own suffering. Were you able to offer love and compassion to those who were seeking your help, your advice, or a moment of your time? Or was your reaction to focus on your own problems and the hurt you were feeling? It takes great strength, a mammoth effort indeed, along with a deep and abiding faith to look past your own needs in order to bring comfort to others. Jesus provided the example of a supreme love. As children of God, we are called to do likewise.

UNISON PRAYER

Forgiving God, in my acts of selfishness I have looked past the needs and hurts of others. I have dismissed their pain and rejected their pleas. In many ways, I have forgotten your commandment to love one another as you have loved me. Forgive my selfish acts and lead me to bring compassion and care to others in their times of need. Your forgiveness is unconditional, and I pray that my love may be the same. Amen.

TWELFTH STATION

Jesus speaks to Mary and John

John 19:25b-27 (THE MESSAGE)

Jesus' mother, his aunt, Mary the wife of Clopas, and Mary Magdalene stood at the foot of the cross. Jesus saw his mother and the disciple he loved standing near her. He said to his mother, "Woman, here is your son." Then to the disciple, "Here is your mother." From that moment the disciple accepted her as his own mother.

REFLECTION

A mother's heart is wracked with pain as she stands at the foot of the cross, watching her son die a horrible, excruciating death. The crown of thorns, blood-spattered nails, and a mocking crowd surely added to the torment she was experiencing. Guilt surely embraced the disciple who was also standing at the foot of the cross, for he had earlier run away in fear. The vastness of God's love and mercy is made real as Jesus forgives in the midst of severe pain. With Jesus' words, John is now given the privilege of caring for Jesus' mother.

UNISON PRAYER

Grant me your grace and mercy, O God. May the example of Mary and John's devotion become my own; let goodness and mercy be hallmarks of my life, and grant me strength to carry out your will in all things. In Jesus' name I pray. Amen.

THIRTEENTH STATION

Jesus dies on the cross

John 19:28-34 (THE MESSAGE)

Jesus, seeing that everything had been completed so that the Scripture record might also be complete, then said, "I'm thirsty."

A jug of sour wine was standing by. Someone put a sponge soaked with the wine on a javelin and lifted it to his mouth. After he took the wine, Jesus said, "It's done . . . complete." Bowing his head, he offered up his spirit.

REFLECTION

Three long, brutal hours nailed to a cross, consumed by pain and suffering, Jesus is now thirsty. Sour wine is offered in scornful response. After a taste, Jesus abandons himself under the weight of his body and the weight of the sins of the world, bows his head, voices "It is finished," and surrenders his spirit to God.

How often we use the phrase "carrying the weight of the world on my shoulders" when faced with some dilemma. The burdens we carry are nothing compared to the tremendous weight that Christ bore on that shameful cross. Imagine, if at all possible, the thoughts that were flashing through Jesus' mind as he hung there facing that coming moment of total surrender.

UNISON PRAYER

O God, there are times when I feel I am carrying the weight of the world on my shoulders, but my burdens are nothing compared to those experienced by Christ

Jesus. Help me, Lord, to surrender my spirit to you that I may walk in your light and love through all my days. Help me to carry the burdens that afflict me in ways that will bring glory to you and may I be found to be a true and faithful disciple. Amen.

FOURTEENTH STATION

Jesus is laid in a tomb

John 19:38-42 (THE MESSAGE)

After all this, Joseph of Arimathea (he was a disciple of Jesus, but secretly, because he was intimidated by the Jews) petitioned Pilate to take the body of Jesus. Pilate gave permission. So Joseph came and took the body.

Nicodemus, who had first come to Jesus at night, came now in broad daylight carrying a mixture of myrrh and aloes, about seventy-five pounds. They took Jesus' body and, following the Jewish burial custom, wrapped it in linens with the spices. There was a garden near the place he was crucified, and in the garden a new tomb in which no one had yet been placed. So, because it was Sabbath preparation for the Jews and the tomb was convenient, they placed Jesus in it.

REFLECTION

Carrying the weight of Jesus' lifeless body must have been a tremendous emotional burden for Joseph and Nicodemus. Finding an unused grave in a garden setting surely brought a measure of comfort to them. It was indeed an honor for them to be accorded the privilege of preparing Jesus' body for burial by wrapping it in linen cloths along with the customary spices. Caring for one they knew and loved in this final act of adoration must have brought relief to their sorrow. Yet, as they walked away from the tomb, the loss was still in their hearts.

When a loved one dies, even though we tend to keep

ourselves busy with all of the necessary preparations, we are still haunted by the loss. Yet, we are comforted by the assurance of God that eternal life is a gift, and we shall meet again one day in God's Holy Kingdom.

UNISON PRAYER

Lord, how difficult it is to imagine your death, but from the other side of the story, we also discover we are people of the resurrection. We are thankful that Jesus traveled the way before us, making God's gift of eternal life possible for all who believe. We thank you, Lord, for the love that Jesus shared and the healing he brought to your people. As we leave this garden of sacred moments and memories, we await the glorious news that "he is not here" but has been risen to eternal life. Thanks be to our God. Amen.

BENEDICTION

Having journeyed the Way of the Cross,
   experiencing the trials and tribulations of our Savior,
   the tears and sorrows and passion of Christ Jesus:
go now into the world aware of the great sacrifice made by our Lord
   to bring salvation to God's people.
Go now in peace. Amen.

EASTER SUNRISE

THEME
God raised Jesus Christ from the tomb, and today we meet our Savior in a garden of love and grace.

GREETING
This morning, this joyous morning, we journey to the tomb with Mary Magdalene and discover the stone is rolled away. An empty grave remains to prove my Savior lives. With joy, we discover that Christ Jesus has risen. Come, let offer praise and thanks to God for fulfilling the resurrection promise.

CALL TO WORSHIP
Christ has risen!
Christ has risen indeed.
Faith, hope, and joy are alive.
A new age is dawning, and death cannot harm us.
God of all creation, we praise you. God of resurrection

and eternal life, we have gathered in this garden to worship you and celebrate your victory.

GATHERING PRAYER

Loving God, we gather in the early morning of your Resurrection. We have been mourning and weeping believing that you have been taken from us. Instead, you meet us in the garden of new life. Here, in this sacred place, we discover that you are alive, that sin and death cannot defeat you. Now our tears of sorrow turn to tears of joy as we experience your presence among us. Today, we begin to understand that joy comes from grief. You call us to go into the world to share this good news, and because we are not left alone, we can pray your prayer. (*All pray the Lord's Prayer.*)

SCRIPTURE READING
JOHN 20:1-18 (*THE MESSAGE*)

Early in the morning on the first day of the week, while it was still dark, Mary Magdalene came to the tomb and saw that the stone was moved away from the entrance. She ran at once to Simon Peter and the other disciple, the one Jesus loved, breathlessly panting, "They took the Master from the tomb. We don't know where they've put him."

Peter and the other disciple left immediately for the tomb. They ran, neck and neck. The other disciple got to the tomb first, outrunning Peter. Stooping to look in, he saw the pieces of linen cloth lying there, but he didn't go in. Simon Peter arrived after him, entered the tomb, observed the linen cloths lying there, and the kerchief used to cover his head not lying with the linen cloths but separate, neatly folded by itself. Then the other disciple, the one who had gotten there first, went into the tomb, took one look at the evidence, and believed. No one yet knew from the Scripture that he had to rise from the dead. The disciples then went back home.

But Mary stood outside the tomb weeping. As she wept, she knelt to look in the tomb and saw two angels sitting there, dressed in white, one at the head, the other at the foot where Jesus' body had been laid. They said to her, "Woman, why do you weep?"

"They took my Master," she said, "and I don't know where they put him." After she said this, she turned away and saw Jesus standing there. But she didn't recognize him.

Jesus spoke to her, "Woman, why do you weep? Who are you looking for?"

She, thinking he was the gardener, said, "Mister, if you took him, tell me where you put him so I can care for him."

Jesus said, "Mary."

Turning to face him, she said in Hebrew, "*Rabboni!*" meaning "Teacher!"

Jesus said, "Don't cling to me, for I have not yet ascended to the Father. Go to my brothers and tell them, 'I ascend to my Father and your Father, my God and your God.'"

Mary Magdalene went, telling the news to the disciples: "I saw the Master!" And she told them everything he said to her.

MEDITATION
IN A GARDEN OF NEW LIFE

It was only a few brief days ago that we were witnesses to the trial, crucifixion, and the death of Jesus. Today, oh how today is so very different.

It all began in a garden: a garden of life, a place of refreshment and renewal. Here, most everything is green with life and growth. We read in the Scriptures that both physical life and eternal life have their genesis in a garden setting. Eve, the mother of humanity, was conceived by God and brought forth in a garden; in fact, it was a lush and vibrant garden of comfort and sanctuary. Yet, because of an act of sheer disobedience, she and her husband, Adam, were expelled from this idyllic paradise. Their lives were cast into a wilderness of despair and death. Paradise was now just a memory.

On this early morning of Easter, we hear of yet another garden. A garden of eternal life made possible through our resurrected Savior, Jesus Christ. Yes, Jesus was crucified, died, and was buried and rose again in a garden setting. Today, we are witnesses to a transformation garden, a resurrection garden.

As we heard in the Gospel reading for this morning, Mary Magdalene is the first to enter this garden, and here, she discovers it was much more than a garden of memories, more than a cemetery to receive the remains of a lifeless body. Mary Magdalene is a principal character in the drama that unfolds in a garden of new life.

Mary Magdalene has returned to this garden of memories to tend to a lifeless body. She is there to more fully prepare and anoint the now dead body of Jesus, but to her amazement, the stone that served to seal the tomb has been rolled away and the body gone, disappeared, nowhere to be found.

No doubt she is panic-stricken, beside herself with fear and worry. In her anxiety and confusion, she runs to Peter and John, and breathlessly panting blurts out, "They took the master from the tomb. We don't know where they've put him." At this moment, she certainly needs a word of confirmation from them. She needs, perhaps more now than ever before, to know that there is a rational explanation for what has taken place. This painful state of unknowing is perhaps the greatest problem she ever faced.

In this dramatic Easter garden account, we too accompany Mary Magdalene and encounter a resurrected Jesus. And, we realize in this experience we encounter once again, that we are the recipients of many, many fruitful blessings. For without that glorious resurrection of Jesus, there would be no hope, no assurance of life eternal. Because he lives, we are provided with the assurance that we will live with him forever and ever. We will live together eternally in the heavenly garden of paradise that God has created. While Mary Magdalene floundered in that garden setting, unknowing, and failing to recognize the resurrected Jesus, we are fortunate to live on the other side of the story. We know the journey Jesus had made, we know the outcome, and we know the hope that abounds.

The Gospel tells us Mary did not recognize Jesus but, rather, thought he was the gardener, a caretaker. How, we wonder, could she not have immediately recognized the one whom she followed and supported and cared for in the days of his earthly ministry? How could she not recognize the one who was so very near and dear to her; the one who chased the demons from her soul, healed her, and forgave her sins? Why, we ask over and over again.

Jesus was different now. He was transformed with a resurrected body that is both physical and spiritual at the same time. We know that when Mary Magdalene finally recognized Jesus and attempted to share an embrace with him, Jesus cautioned, "Don't cling to me, for I have not yet ascended to the Father." The same holds true for us also. As Paul taught, when Christians die, they are transformed with a similar body—spiritual, imperishable, eternal.

Mary Magdalene didn't remain in that garden with the resurrected and transformed Jesus. Her encounter with Jesus created so much excitement that she knew she must share this good news with others. Full of wonder, full of hope, she again raced to Peter and John and boldly exclaimed, "I have seen the Master!"

For Mary Magdalene, Peter, and John, and for all who follow in the footsteps of Jesus, it was simply the best news ever heard. Yes, Easter is the most glorious day of the year. It is the day we celebrate the joyous news that the Master is alive, that a new, transformed life has blossomed in a garden.

Because Christ Jesus defeated death, he is truly the victorious one. And by his victory, we are given the wonderful promise, "Because I live, you also will live!"

Thanks be to God!

CLOSING PRAYER (UNISON)

Lord, we have so much to be thankful for this Easter morning. In the chill of the morning air, we do feel the warm blessing of your Spirit. We can rejoice this day because our tendency toward disbelief is overcome by our capacity for faith. We are truly amazed that a cross of crucifixion has been transformed into a symbol of new life, a symbol of eternal life.

We are thankful that you come to greet us in a garden of hope, trust, and faith. We thank you that a dark and empty tomb has emerged into a garden of light and living. In all our days, we shall live for Christ, the resurrected and risen Savior. Amen.

BENEDICTION

The tomb is empty,
    Christ has risen.
As you journey in faith,
    may your life be full,
    your love be abundant,
    and your hope be eternal.
Live this day and always for Christ Jesus
    because the Risen Christ lives in you.
Alleluia! Christ is Risen!

BLESSING OF THE ANIMALS

THEME

God's divine creation includes the birds of the air, the fish of the sea, and all the animals that walk this earth.

GREETING

Welcome! People of God. Welcome! Pets of God's creation. Today is a special day in the life of this congregation. We gather together, along with our pets, to honor and bless their being, thankful for their days with us offering comfort, protection, and the wonderful gift of companionship. May this service of celebration be a meaningful moment in our time together.

GATHERING PRAYER (UNISON)

Gracious God, we gather on this joyous occasion to celebrate and honor the pets in our lives. In your wisdom, you created the universe and blessed us with living creatures. We are grateful that you have entrusted their care to us. May they continue to bring us immense joy and comfort in all our days together. Help us to be good and faithful stewards of your creation, and may we always find joy and wonder in your gifts. Especially this day, we remember those pets who have passed on. We hold the memories of them deep within our hearts. Give us a greater sense of responsibility in the care and nurture of all your creation. Amen.

SCRIPTURE READING
GENESIS 2:19B-20A; PROVERBS 12:10
(*THE MESSAGE*)

GOD said, "It's not good for the Man to be alone; I'll make him a helper, a companion." So GOD formed from the dirt of the ground all the animals of the field and the birds of the air. He brought them to the Man to see what he would name them. Whatever the Man called each living creature, that was its name. The Man named the cattle, named the birds of the air, named the wild animals.

And from the Book of Proverbs, chapter 12, verse 10, we hear these words:

Good people are good to their animals;
    the "good-hearted" bad people kick and abuse them.

MEDITATION

What are you hearing today? Today we are hearing some unfamiliar sounds, sounds that we're not used to hearing in a worship service. Today, this garden is filled with a symphony of unusual sounds: barking, meowing, chirping, and so much more. These delightful sounds—sounds that are quite normal in our homes—have joined us today in praise of God and all of God's creation. In fact, their praise is likely to be much more spontaneous and exuberant than we normally witness. These creatures of God may, in fact, sing, dance, run, romp, cavort, and cele-brate life in ways true to their species. Their acts of praise may be different than ours, different than what we are used to, yet it is divine praise nonetheless.

I have found over the years that when it comes to people and their pets, there's a whole lot of talk about unconditional love. People often remind me how our pets love us without reservation. They love us no matter how well or how poorly we treat them. They love us in much the same way that God loves the human and the animal species. I'm certain that every pet owner here today knows what I'm speaking about.

Living alone as a poor beggar among God's creation, Saint Francis saw God as the absolute source of everything that lives, of creatures great and small. In fact, Francis envisioned God as the divine link between humans, animals, plants, the seas, the sun, moon, and stars. Saint Francis, even at an early age, understood that the earth and all its fullness is of the Lord and that we are charged with caring for everything created by God, everything that belongs to God.

The Old Testament reading from the Genesis account of creation links us with animals in a wonderful array of ways. Not only are we all creatures of God's handiwork and inhabitants of this Earth but we also are essentially made from the same stuff as animals. Do we not also breathe the same air? And that being true, are we not also inhaling the same breath or Spirit of God?

In forming this vast cosmos, God created a garden on Earth and along with Adam, placed the animals in that garden as part of the family of living creatures. We are here together, to share in all of the beauty of God's creation—humans and animals–in partnership, as companions, to bring praise to God. God's creative power is illustrated dramatically in every single facet of creation. And so, the challenge for us today is to recognize, respect, and revere all of God's creation, by being kind to one another, offering Godlike unconditional love, and offering praise to our Creator.

ACT OF BLESSING/ANOINTING

The gathering may bring their pets forward for a blessing and anointing.

Bless, O Lord, *(name of animal)* and fill the hearts of its owners with thanksgiving for the companionship of this pet, and the love and protection it provides.

PRAYER OF REMEMBRANCE

As I look out over this gathering, I see several people carrying urns containing the remains of their pets that have passed beyond this world. I invite those owners to come forward for a prayer of remembrance.

Lord God, our Creator, you have shared with us the lives of these pets who have now departed from their earthly journey. They have given us a sense of companionship and shared with us their love and affection. They have brought us great joy and much laughter. We thank you, Lord, for our time together. We hold their memories in our hearts and pray that you will now care for them in your eternal realm. Amen.

DISMISSAL WITH BLESSING

Go as instruments of God's peace; go as a steward and caretaker of God's divine creation. May the God who created the animals of this earth continue to protect and sustain us all, now and forever. Amen.

HEALING SERVICE

The garden typically provides a calming place of restoration and healing. A simple gathering invokes not only a keen sense of fellowship but also a greater sense of hospitality and caring as we seek to be made whole through God's healing touch.

THEME
We journey in faith and seek to touch the hem of Jesus' garment for healing and wholeness.

GREETING
Trust GOD from the bottom of your heart;
    don't try to figure out everything on your own.
Listen for GOD's voice in everything you do, everywhere you go;
    he's the one who will keep you on track.
Don't assume that you know it all.
    Run to GOD! Run from evil!
Your body will glow with health,
    your very bones will vibrate with life!
Proverbs 3:5-8 (THE MESSAGE)

GATHERING PRAYER (UNISON)

Gracious, Loving and Merciful God, as we gather together to worship you, we come knowing that your love reaches out to all people. Your love is unconditional, shared as a gift of grace. Open our minds, Lord, touch our hearts, and make us more receptive to your Spirit. You are the Divine Healer, and we approach you with needs and concerns, for ourselves and for others. Look favorably upon us as we seek your healing touch. Allow us as we journey in faith, to partake of your strength, your love, and your promise of abundant and eternal life. Cleanse our hearts, minds, and spirits that we may be transformed by your Word and by your Will. This we pray in Jesus' name. Amen.

SCRIPTURE READINGS
MATTHEW 9:18-26 (*THE MESSAGE*)

A reading from Matthew's Gospel, chapter 9, verses 18 through 26. We hear of two miraculous healings taking place.

As he finished saying this, a local official appeared, bowed politely, and said, "My daughter has just now died. If you come and touch her, she will live." Jesus got up and went with him, his disciples following along.

Just then a woman who had hemorrhaged for twelve years slipped in from behind and lightly touched his robe. She was thinking to herself, "If I can just put a finger on his robe, I'll get well." Jesus turned—caught her at it. Then he reassured her, "Courage, daughter. You took a risk of faith, and now you're well." The woman was well from then on.

By now they had arrived at the house of the town official, and pushed their way through the gossips looking for a story and the neighbors bringing in casseroles. Jesus was abrupt: "Clear out! This girl isn't dead. She's sleeping." They told him he didn't know what he was talking about. But when Jesus had gotten rid of the crowd, he went in, took the girl's hand, and pulled her to her feet—alive. The news was soon out, and traveled throughout the region.

MEDITATION

We gather today in a garden, essentially chosen because a garden is often regarded as a place of healing. Many times when someone feels troubled, the garden becomes a place of respite, renewal, and refreshment. We are here today to pray, anoint the sick, and to worship God as our Creator and the ultimate source of our healing and wholeness. We are here also in testimony to the words of James, who said in chapter 5, verses 13 through 16:

Are you hurting? Pray. Do you feel great? Sing. Call the church leaders together to pray and anoint you with oil in the name of the Master. Believing-prayer will heal you, and Jesus will put you on your feet. And if you've sinned, you'll be forgiven—healed inside and out.

Make this your common practice: Confess your sins to each other and pray for each other so that you can live together whole and healed. The prayer of a person living right with God is something powerful to be reckoned with.

From the very beginning, the ministry of healing has played a pivotal and vital role in the life of the Church of Jesus Christ. There are a goodly number of healing accounts found in sacred scripture, healings performed by Christ Jesus, the apostles, and by the disciples that were later sent out to preach and heal, even to raise the dead.

In the passage of scripture, we heard read a few moments ago, not one, but two powerful stories of healing take place. First, we find Jairus, a local official and leader of the synagogue, coming to Jesus with news that his daughter has just died. Looking beyond the mere words of the text, we can hear Jairus' pleading voice of determined faith: "If you come and touch her, she will live." Jairus pleads for Jesus to come to his house, lay hands on her, and return her to life. The pain and anguish that Jairus must have been feeling was no doubt overwhelming. He is ready to try any means to bring his daughter back to life. He is frantic, on the edge of sanity.

Jesus agrees to Jairus' plea, and they are on their way when Jesus is once again called on to bring about a healing miracle. As Jesus is moving through a crowd of people, a woman who has suffered from hemorrhages for many years quietly pushes her way toward Jesus, hoping desperately to touch him. With but a touch of his garment, she truly believes she will be healed of her infirmity. Deep in her heart of faith, she trusts the power of Jesus to bring healing to her broken body; through Jesus, God will heal her. She reaches out to Jesus, and a miracle occurs! A deep sensation is felt, and she is completely focused on the healing taking place.

Yet, something else quite dramatic happens. Jesus has also felt that touch, turns to the woman, and reassures her, "Courage, daughter. You took a risk of faith, and now you're well." What a comfort to hear Jesus reassure her. What a connection she has made, and now she is healed. As James suggests, there is wonder-working power in prayer; believing-prayer will heal you. Our prayers for healing are a reaching out to Jesus, a reaching out to touch the hem of his garment.

Following this miraculous healing experience, the original problem of Jairus' daughter once again reasserts itself. Jesus meets a crowd while arriving at Jairus' house, crowds of people looking for a bit of gossip to spread, crowds of onlookers hungry to see this miracle worker in action. Jesus seems to burst their bubble when he sternly instructs, "Clear out! This girl isn't dead. She's sleeping." Disappointed, the crowd disperses rather quickly, and Jesus enters the house with Jairus. He takes the girl's hand and pulls her to her feet. She's alive. Jesus now reaches out, touches the girl, and she is brought to life. Once dead, the girl now lives again.

As we are gathered here today, will we, in deep and abiding faith, reach out to touch Jesus? Do we believe in the wonder-working power of prayer and invite God to reach out to offer a healing touch to remedy our ills, our brokenness, our pain and hurt? Through prayer, make that connection with the Divine and experience God's mystery of healing, praying that God's will be done in your life.

PRAYER OF CONFESSION (UNISON)
Lord God, you are the way of healing, hope, and renewal.
Enter our broken lives and uncover our sinfulness.
In our lack of trust and the fears we embrace,
   we miss the miracles of your healing presence,
   the generosity of your love and grace,
   that heals our brokenness and restores our faith.
Forgive, restore, and renew each one of us,
   in the name of Christ Jesus. Amen.
Open our eyes, our ears, and our hearts to your mercy
   that we might be your faithful disciples.

ASSURANCE OF PARDON
Hear the Good News!
Christ died for your sins, and for your healing.
In the name of Jesus Christ you are forgiven!
Praise be to God, our Creator and Healer.

PRAYER OF THANKSGIVING OVER THE OIL
Precious Lord, Creator and Healer,
   we give you thanks for the gift of oil
   and for your healing message.
We hear the stories of how your disciples followed your lead,
   went into the world, and healed many who were sick.
   Pour out your Holy Spirit to bless this oil

that those who journey in faith, repent of their sins,
and receive this anointing may be healed and made
whole;
We pray this blessing in Jesus' precious name. Amen.

PRAYER FOR HEALING

Following the example taught by James, you are invited to
come forward for healing prayers. If desired, you may also
receive an anointing and laying on of hands. You may come for
personal healing or on behalf of another person. In faith, hope,
and trust, join us at the altar of God's forgiveness and grace.

Those desiring prayer may come forward. One at a time,
each person is to be greeted, a prayer request is privately
shared, and quiet prayer offered while hands are laid on
the person. A sign of the cross using oil of healing may
then be administered to the person's forehead.

CLOSING PRAYER (UNISON)

**Gracious and loving God, we thank you for the bless-
ing of healing and wholeness received this day. We thank
you for searching out our pain, removing our fears, and
forgiving our sins. Help each one of us to be refreshed by
the anointing of your Holy Spirit to go forth to give ourselves for others, and to be your healing presence in the
world today. In the name of Jesus we pray. Amen.**

BENEDICTION

Go forth from this garden of healing
as one made whole in the name of Jesus;
Go forth as a reflection of God's
love, forgiveness, and hope.
Go in peace. **Amen.**

REFLECTION,
RECONCILIATION,
AND RENEWAL

THEME

As weeds and thorns are removed from the garden, renewed, stronger life emerges; so it is with our relationships.

GREETING

Christ Jesus seeks a spirit of peace and a sense of unity in the world. For that reason, we gather to reflect on our brokenness, reconcile the many differences that may be taking place in our lives, and experience a renewal of relations so that we may truly be a blessing to God, our Creator. Healing the wounds that divide us creates a tie that binds us together as the Body of Christ. This is a day that the Lord has made; let us rejoice and experience God's love given so freely.

CALL TO WORSHIP

In Christ is our unity,
    in Christ is our wholeness.
Thanks be to God!
In Christ is our forgiveness,
    in Christ is our reconciliation and renewal.
**Thanks be to God, for grace offered and grace
received.**

PRAYER OF CONFESSION (UNISON)

O God,
we confess the things we attempt to hide from you,
the things we strive to hide from others,
and the many things we often hide from ourselves.
We confess the anger and frustration
    we have caused others and
    the things we have said and done
    that make it difficult for them to offer forgiveness.
We confess the times we have made it easy for others
to sin,
    to feel betrayed, and encouraged others to be
resentful.
We also confess the great harm we have done in other
people's lives,
    often in very selfish and self-centered ways.
Lord, we pray for your mercy and ask your
forgiveness.

DECLARATION OF GOD'S FORGIVENESS

If we confess and truly repent of our sins,
God is faithful and just and will offer forgiveness.
God will cleanse us from words and acts of
unrighteousness.
Hear then Christ's word of grace to each of us:
Your sins are forgiven; be cleansed and made whole.
Response: **Thanks be to God.**

PASSING OF THE PEACE

SCRIPTURE READINGS
EZEKIEL 47:1-2, 12; REVELATION 22:1-7
(*THE MESSAGE*)

A reading from the Old Testament book of Ezekiel, chapter 47, verses 1 and 2 and verse 12 and a reading from Revelation, chapter 22, verses 1 through 7. Hear now the Word of God.

Now he brought me back to the entrance to the Temple. I saw water pouring out from under the Temple porch to the east (the Temple faced east). The water poured from the south side of the Temple, south of the altar. He then took me out through the north gate and led me around the outside to the gate complex on the east. The water was gushing from under the south front of the Temple.

But the river itself, on both banks, will grow fruit trees of all kinds. Their leaves won't wither, the fruit won't fail. Every month they'll bear fresh fruit because the river from the Sanctuary flows to them. Their fruit will be for food and their leaves for healing.

Then the Angel showed me Water-of-Life River, crystal bright. It flowed from the Throne of God and the Lamb, right down the middle of the street. The Tree of Life was planted on each side of the River, producing twelve kinds of fruit, a ripe fruit each month. The leaves of the Tree are for the healing of the nations. Never again will anything be cursed. The Throne of God and of the Lamb is at the center. His servants will offer God service—worshiping, they'll look on his face, their foreheads mirroring God. Never again will there be any night. No one will need lamplight or sunlight. The shining of God, the Master, is all the light anyone needs. And they will rule with him age after age after age.

This is the Word of God for the people of God.

MEDITATION
BRIDGE OVER TROUBLED WATERS

Then the Angel showed me Water-of-Life River, crystal bright—a verse from Revelation visualizing the promised paradise: our lives together with the final coming of Christ as we journey through the gates of heaven. The river is pure, crystal bright we are told. How beautiful a portrait John reveals of the New Jerusalem. In fact, there are many verses in scripture that tell of the beauty and symbolism of the river of life.

At its base is the river that watered the Garden of Eden and made it fruitful, as the book of Genesis so vividly describes. The psalmist sings of the "River fountains splash joy, cooling GOD's city" (Psalm 46:4 *THE MESSAGE*). "A fountain," says the prophet Joel, "shall come forth from the house of the LORD" (Joel 3:18b). "God," said the rabbis in their dream of the golden age, "will produce a river from the Holy of Holies, beside which every kind of delicate fruit will grow." And from the Gospel of John, Jesus teaches, "Rivers of living water will brim and spill out of the depths of anyone who believes in me" (John 7:38 *THE MESSAGE*). And I would add, Jesus is the ever-flowing fountain that keeps my soul alive and satisfied.

In reading and meditating on these passages of Scripture, I began to visualize a sort of pristine garden setting— a beautiful autumn morning, surrounded by God's creation; a ray of warm sunlight penetrating the morning chill; sipping a hot cup of coffee; perhaps a cool, clear stream flowing nearby.

Today, however, when we step outside the idyllic gardens of our mind, the river of life is not the majestic, serene picture that John so dramatically described. Often this river runs murky, with a scary swiftness, tainted by the impurities of human life itself, made impure by our greed and selfish ways.

Our journey along this river is often filled with sadness, fear, confusion, and pain. And as we're swept along in its raging currents, it becomes so easy to be overtaken by those negative forces that creep into our existence. So often we are weak, vulnerable, or downright afraid and allow the storms of life—the troubled waters—to rule our emotions, our thoughts, our very being.

As this unfortunate chain of events takes place, it becomes more and more difficult to ford those troubled waters and continue along the path of life with a bright, optimistic outlook. We fail to allow ourselves to grow and blossom as God would will.

We, as human beings, can become so totally immersed in our fears, our problems, our pain and hurts—the raging waters—that it becomes absolutely necessary to fight desperately to reach the safety and security of the opposite shore. At times, the waters are so murky, so polluted, so rapid and wild, that we lose all hope of recovery and then drown in our own fear and misery.

It is only with total, uncompromising faith in Jesus the Christ that we can bridge these troubled waters and continue on a positive, meaningful journey through life. At times, we are hurt by others in word or deed, and as we reflect on these troubling experiences and bridge their stormy currents, only then are we able to experience genuine reconciliation and renewal.

While reading the passage from Revelation, I was reminded—quite vividly—of a popular song from my past. The song by Paul Simon and Art Garfunkel is called "Bridge Over Troubled Water." I'm certain you've heard its captivating music and listened to its encouraging words many, many times.

Thinking back to my early years and hearing those words, I remember playing that record over and over again, intently listening to the message it was speaking to me, somehow captivated by what I was hearing. Something was moving my spirit, and I just couldn't put my finger on what it was. I remember trying to analyze and somehow decipher the words, trying to discover some hidden meaning behind the lyrics. I realized, however, that I was focusing much too hard, analyzing way too much, digging much too deep.

In a truly delightful way, I have come to believe there is a vital message in these words: a message which can act as a bridge in our sometimes troubled lives. Just as these words seemed to have said to me—or perhaps my own unique interpretation of them—there is an undeniable bridge over our troubled waters. A power so strong, so positive that there should be no doubt in our minds that any river of troubled water can be a bridge, carrying us back to the solid rock, the mighty foundation that created us. This divine bridge can carry us over all of those negative experiences, all of the hurt and pain that might be caused by others, and all of those negative desires in our lives. Traversing this bridge will allow us to move on in life, in relationships, in our pain and hurts with a new and profound sense of strength, hope, love, and a more positive outlook. That divine bridge known as Jesus Christ will ease our minds.

When you feel weary or small, when times are rough, when tears flow like rivers, Jesus is the bridge to healing and wholeness. When you're overcome by life's demands and feeling so down and out, when darkness surrounds you like a clouded sky, Jesus is that bridge that will take away your pain. Feeling lost, alone, helpless, or hopeless, Jesus is the bridge to fellowship and friendship.

"Like a bridge over troubled water, I will lay me down." Jesus Christ, Lord and Savior, did indeed lay down his life for us. Jesus came and laid down his own life not only that we may live but that the life we live may be more abundant. Even with the veil of threat hanging over us, with the pangs of fear driving our lives, with the feelings of hurt and pain cause by others overwhelming our being, our souls can be filled with God's redeeming love. In accepting Christ's forgiveness and gift of love, we may be cleansed by the gentle, crystal bright rivers which flow that the throne of God.

Yes, it's true, so very true, that Christ Jesus has the positive power to wrap us in his Spirit, give us direction, and comfort us from those tormenting, pain-filled moments hat so often overtake our lives. Jesus desires to be that bridge over our troubled waters—those waters that seemingly run with a scary swiftness; a dark, foreboding murkiness may seem to cloud the future.

Friends, as we celebrate a ritual of reconciliation and renewal this day, why not invite Jesus to be that bridge that when crossed will lead you to the living waters? Invite Jesus to be that bridge to faith, hope, love, and eternal life.

ACT OF RECONCILIATION AND RENEWAL

A brazier or urn may be placed in the garden setting, to be used as a receptacle for the placement and disposal of "forgiveness" cards. The cards may be handed out to all participants at the beginning of the service.

> Healing • Forgiveness • Reconciliation
>
> *Is there someone in your life you need to forgive?*
> *You can experience the freedom God offers by praying:*
> "God, I am angry and hurt because of what
> _____ did to me. I don't feel like
> forgiving, and in my own strength, I know I
> can't. But because you have freely forgiven me, I
> now choose to forgive. Today, by your grace I
> will begin accepting _____, and will
> seek to restore our broken relationship.
>
> _____

At this time, the pastor may invite participants to complete the information requested on the card and then place it in the brazier to burn. If an urn is used, after all cards are deposited, the pastor or worship leader may set fire to the deposited cards and indicate that the ritual is meant to be a time of new beginnings and from the ashes a renewal of relationships may be experienced.

SACRAMENT OF HOLY COMMUNION

It would be most appropriate to share in the Sacrament of Holy Communion at this time. The Invitation, Great Thanksgiving, and Prayers should certainly make reference to acts of forgiveness, reconciliation, and renewal.

PRAYER AFTER COMMUNION (UNISON)

O Christ, our one and only Savior,
    dwell with each of us that we may go forward
    as vessels of your faith, hope, and love.
May we move on from this time of reflection
    feeling the gift of your forgiveness,
    the blessing of reconciliation, and
    joyously sharing the experience of renewal.
Amen.

CELEBRATION OF FORGIVENESS

God calls us to forgive one another as God forgives each one of us. Let us now offer one another the peace of Jesus Christ.

DEPARTING PRAYER

Oh God, this day has been a profound, emotional experience for each of us gathered in this sanctuary garden. May it be that we have finally released the hurt and pain we believe was caused by others—family members, friends, co-workers or neighbors. When trouble abounds in our lives, may we look to Jesus to be that bridge that will lift us out of harm's way and over the troubling waters that seem to rage around us. Help us each, Lord, to experience a true sense of reconciliation and renewal as we go forth from this place. This we pray in Jesus' name. Amen.

DISMISSAL WITH BLESSING

Go now in peace from our time of reflection, reconciliation, and renewal, joyously sharing a sense of hope and love. Go forth with faith and grace in your hearts and the light of Christ's love in your eyes. Forgive one another as Christ has freely forgiven each one of us and then allow Jesus to be your bridge over the troubles you may face. **Amen.**

LOVE FEAST

The Love Feast (Agape Meal) is a recalling of the
meals Jesus shared with his disciples, and further
serves to express the spirit of hospitality, community,
and fellowship that is enjoyed by the family of Christ.
The service allows for the gathered people to hear what
God is doing in people's lives. This is accomplished by
the sharing of joys and concerns and the offering of testimonies of God's movement and blessings in people's
lives. It must be cautioned that the Love Feast is not to be
confused with the Sacrament of Communion, although
Communion may be celebrated at the conclusion of the
Love Feast service.

Within a garden setting, the Love Feast is perhaps best
experienced while seated in a circle. At the center of the
circle may be placed a small table to accommodate coffee,
tea, juices, and water, as well as an assortment of home-
made baked goods. The gathering of people should be
invited to serve themselves from the refreshment table as
the need arises, throughout the service.

THEME

Celebrating the gifts of God's hospitality and witnessing to our faith in appreciation for God's multitude of blessing.

GREETING

Jesus said, "People will come from the east and west and north and south, and will take their places at the feast in the kingdom of God" (Luke 13:29 NIV). As children of God, we are all invited to this heavenly banquet. As a community of faith, we are encouraged to lift our prayers for one another, share our concerns with one another, and rejoice in one another's joys and accomplishments. We do this as a sign of God's outpouring of blessings and the movement of God's Holy Spirit in our lives.

One of God's first acts was to create a garden, a garden designed for life, peace, and unity. Today, we gather in a God-given garden to celebrate not only the love that God shares with each one of us but also to witness to our faith in a ritual of sharing and fellowship.

GATHERING PRAYER (UNISON)

Loving and caring God, as we are gathered together in this caring circle of fellowship, we thank you for your abundant grace and for the love you share. We rejoice in the gift of your Holy Spirit that both nurtures and nourishes us and calls us to extend that same gift of hospitality to our neighbor. We have tasted and savored your many blessings as we journey through life and truly await the blessing of your heavenly feast.

We thank you, Lord, for the precious gift of your Son, Jesus, sent into this world to live with us, as one of us, to eat and drink and laugh and cry with us, to pray for us and love us so that we might have a foretaste of your promise of eternal life.

God, let your love and your light continue to shine in and through us so that we may be the image of Christ in

the world today. Teach us to share the love, grace, mercy, and peace that you so freely give. May we always live in gratitude for the gift of your Son, Jesus, who taught us to pray using these words:

Our Father, who art in heaven,
hallowed be thy name.
Thy kingdom come,
thy will be done on earth as it is in heaven.
Give us this day our daily bread.
And forgive us our trespasses,
as we forgive those who trespass against us.
And lead us not into temptation,
but deliver us from evil.
For thine is the kingdom and the power,
and the glory, forever. Amen.

SCRIPTURE READING

Numerous passages of scripture are appropriate for sharing in the Love Feast. Several passages may also be interspersed throughout the service. Basic suggestions include:

OLD TESTAMENT READING
PSALM 145:8-21 (*THE MESSAGE*)

GOD is all mercy and grace—
not quick to anger, is rich in love.
GOD is good to one and all;
everything he does is suffused with grace,
Creation and creatures applaud you, GOD;
your holy people bless you.
They talk about the glories of your rule,
they exclaim over your splendor,
Letting the world know of your power for good,
the lavish splendor of your kingdom.
Your kingdom is a kingdom eternal;

you never get voted out of office.
GOD always does what he says,
 and is gracious in everything he does.
GOD gives a hand to those down on their luck,
 gives a fresh start to those ready to quit.
All eyes are on you, expectant;
 you give them their meals on time.
Generous to a fault
 you lavish your favor on all creatures.
Everything GOD does is right—
 the trademark on all his works is love.
GOD's there, listening to all who pray,
 for all who pray and mean it.
He does what's best for those who fear him—
 hears them call out, and saves them.
GOD sticks by all those who love him,
 but it's all over for those who don't.
My mouth is filled with GOD 's praise.
 Let everything living bless him,
 bless his holy name from now to eternity!

EPISTLE READING
2 CORINTHIANS 9:6-15 (*THE MESSAGE*)

Remember: A stingy planter gets a stingy crop; a lavish planter gets a lavish crop. I want each of you to take plenty of time to think it over, and make up your own mind what you will give. That will protect you against sob stories and arm-twisting. God loves it when the giver delights in the giving.

God can pour on the blessings in astonishing ways so that you're ready for anything and everything, more than just ready to do what needs to be done. As one psalmist puts it:

He throws caution to the winds,
 giving to the needy in reckless abandon.
His right-living, right-giving ways
 never run out, never wear out.

This most generous God who gives seed to the farmer that becomes bread for your meals is more than extravagant with you. He gives you something you can then give away, which grows into full-formed lives, robust in God, wealthy in every way, so that you can become generous in every way, producing with us great praise to God.

Carrying out this social relief work involves far more than helping meet the bare needs of poor Christians. It also produces abundant and bountiful thanksgivings to God. This relief offering is a prod to live at your very best, showing your gratitude to God by being openly obedient to the plain meaning of the Message of Christ. You show your gratitude through your generous offerings to your needy brothers and sisters and, really, toward everyone. Meanwhile, moved by the extravagance of God in your lives, they'll respond by praying for you in passionate intercession for whatever you need. Thank God for this gift, his gift. No language can praise it enough!

GOSPEL READING
JOHN 6:25-35 (*THE MESSAGE*)

When they found him back across the sea, they said, "Rabbi, when did you get here?"

Jesus answered, "You've come looking for me not because you saw God in my actions but because I fed you, filled your stomachs—and for free.

"Don't waste your energy striving for perishable food like that. Work for the food that sticks with you, food that nourishes your lasting life, food the Son of Man provides. He and what he does are guaranteed by God the Father to last."

To that they said, "Well, what do we do then to get in on God's works?"

Jesus said, "Throw your lot in with the One that God has sent. That kind of a commitment gets you in on God's works."

They waffled, "Why don't you give us a clue about who

you are, just a hint of what's going on? When we see what's up, we'll commit ourselves. Show us what you can do. Moses fed our ancestors with bread in the desert. It says so in the scriptures: 'He gave them bread from heaven to eat.'"

Jesus responded, "The real significance of that Scripture is not that Moses gave you bread from heaven but that my Father right now is offering you bread from heaven, the *real* bread. The Bread of God came down out of heaven and is giving life to this world."

They jumped at that: "Master, give us this bread, now and forever!"

Jesus said, "I am the Bread of Life. The person who aligns with me hungers no more and thirsts no more, ever."

SHARING JOYS AND CONCERNS

The assembly is invited to briefly share some of the joys and accomplishments they have celebrated or are presently experiencing. Prayer requests for concerns of the people are also invited at this time.

Following the time of sharing, prayers are offered by the worship leader in thanksgiving for the joys and accomplishments noted, as well as prayers addressing the concerns raised. A brief time of silent reflection following the prayer would be most appropriate.

Upon completion of the prayers of the people, a reminder to partake of refreshments should once again be extended.

WITNESS TO FAITH AND DISCIPLESHIP

Testimonies celebrating God's movement in people's lives may be offered, focusing on the ways in which one's faith has grown and matured, or on how God has empowered a participant to become a disciple and serve the Lord in unexpected ways. Again, testimonies should be brief and general in nature.

PRAYER OF THANKSGIVING

Lord of love and grace,
>we thank you for all that has been,
>>all that is, and all that is to be.

We hear the stories of Jesus sharing meals and fellowship with his disciples
>and remember how the Lord added to their numbers.

We hear stories of joy and celebration
>and concerns that speak to our hearts.

In our gathering, we celebrate your love,
>your care and compassion,
>>and pray that we may live as faithful witnesses
>>in the world today.

Empower us, O God, through the gift of your Spirit,
>to teach others of your embracing love
>>through our acts of love, truth, justice, and devotion.

This we pray in Jesus' name. Amen.

DISMISSAL WITH BLESSING

Go now, from this garden of God's creation
>to love God and your neighbor in all your words and acts.

Go in peace, and may the love of God bless you,
>the joy of Christ embrace you,
>>and the nurturing of the Holy Spirit lead you in faith.

Be the light and love of God to a broken world.

Amen.

WEDDING

THEME

Man and Woman became one in the garden of creation. Today, a man and a woman stand in a garden of love and are united in the covenant of marriage.

GATHERING PRAYER

Loving God,
    long, long ago, in the garden of creation,
you formed from the earth man and woman for each other.
Let your blessing be upon this couple
    as they pledge their love and faith to one another.
May our time of sharing in this garden,
    give us a joyous sense of wonder
    and a renewed spirit of love. Amen.

GREETING

On behalf of (*bride's name*) and (*groom's name*) and their families,

I welcome you to this celebration of marriage.

Today, this couple stands before God and this congregation,

to publicly give their marriage vows to one another.

We are here as witnesses to these vows

and to celebrate with (*bride's name*) and (*groom's name*)

their love and affection for one another.

Let us, together, worship God.

OPENING PRAYER
(TYPICALLY FOLLOWS THE CHARGE TO THE COUPLE/DECLARATION OF INTENT)

Loving and Creating God,

from our beginnings in the Garden of Eden,

you created us to be loving and fruitful.

The beauty of your creation surrounds us today,

as we feel your Spirit embracing us in love.

We pray, O God, that you would shower this couple with blessings,

that their love for one another would grow and blossom

much like a seed planted in fertile soil.

Nourish them as they grow, nurture them with care and compassion,

and may they be beautiful examples of a constantly flowering love.

Amen.

SCRIPTURE READING
GENESIS 2:18, 21-24 (*THE MESSAGE*)

GOD said, "It's not good for Man to be alone; I'll make him a helper, a companion."

GOD put the Man into a deep sleep. As he slept he removed one of his ribs and replaced it with flesh. GOD then used the rib that he had taken from the Man to make Woman and presented her to the Man.

The Man said,

"Finally! Bone of my bone,
    flesh of my flesh!
Name her Woman
    for she was made from Man."

Therefore a man leaves his father and mother and embraces his wife. They become one flesh.

MEDITATION
LOVE BLOSSOMS IN A GARDEN

A little girl grows up with the dream of being married in a beautiful garden setting, surrounded by a vibrant palette of colors, textures, and aromas. Today this very dream is being realized as we gather with (*bride's name*) and (*groom's name*) as they pledge their love and faith to one another. What a sheer joy it is for all of us as we see the seed of God's love bearing fruit this day.

(*Bride's name*) and (*groom's name*), as you are aware, this garden in which you stand is a very special place in the hearts and minds of the congregation that worships here. In fact, many of them regard this garden as a holy and sacred creation of God. So, it is most fitting that you have chosen this setting for the celebration of your marriage. Your love, a love that began much like that of a tiny seed, has now grown and blossomed into a life-giving plant of God's creation.

The miracle of your love is much like the miracle of this garden; it will require constant care and devout attention for it to grow and fully mature. Most important, it is through the nurturing of one another that you will, undoubtedly, discover the fullness of life through the joys of caring and sharing. And, as your love continues to grow, your roots will become more and more secured in the precious memories of days gone by. In much the same way, you will surely begin to experience, and then eagerly anticipate, the promise of many more joy-filled tomorrows together. As in a garden, one constantly remembers the beauty of the flowers of past years and looks forward to the surprises of a whole new season.

We are here on this festive occasion to not only rejoice with you but also to remind you both that in your life together you will experience seasons much like this garden. There will be periods of growth and seasons of loss. Your love, at times, will grow and exhibit signs of wondrous springtime beauty. At other times, it may seem as if your love is like a dormant seed buried under the snows of winter: resting, yet gaining newfound strength to grow and blossom. All these seasons of feelings and emotions will be yours to have and to hold; they will, in fact, be your life together.

Above all else, (bride's name) and (groom's name), I caution that you cannot grow the garden of your love and marriage on your own. Every beautiful garden has a gardener to cultivate and maintain the plantings so as to bring out the richness and fullness of the garden. With Christ Jesus at the center of your lives your marriage will surely reap a bountiful harvest. You will truly enjoy the fruits of your labor as you become the new creation that God intends for you. With Christ Jesus as the Master Gardener of your individual lives, and your lives together, your marriage will be nurtured, sustained, and filled with the bounty of God's blessings.

So, dear (bride's name) and (groom's name), our hope and prayer for you today is that you will remember the image of the garden in your lives together. With God nurturing and nourishing your marriage, you will certainly blossom in love, truth, and beauty. May it always be so. Amen.

EXCHANGE OF VOWS

(Groom's name), I ask you to repeat after me:
(Bride's name), as we stand together

in this garden of God's creation,
your beauty blossoms like a fragrant rose,
and my being flowers
because of your love.
Because of you, my life is brand new.
I give myself, my love, my being to you
freely and wholly this day,
to be your loving and faithful husband,
so we may share our lives together,
as long as our Creator allows.

(*Bride's name*), I also ask you to repeat after me:
(*Groom's name*), as we stand together
in this garden of God's creation,
your love has nourished my soul,
and allowed me to blossom into wholeness.
Because of your love, my life is also brand new.
I give myself, my love, my being to you
freely and completely this day,
to be your loving and faithful wife,
so long as our Creator allows.

RITUAL OF UNITY
A ROSE RITUAL

Many couples are now seeking meaningful alternatives to the more traditional unity candle ceremony. Within a garden setting a number of options are available and appropriate. The Rose Ritual or Ceremony is one such option.

In a Rose Ceremony, each partner offers the other a single rose as a symbol and token of their love, and each partner makes the promise to use a red rose as a symbol of their shared love through the years to come.

Officiant:

The red rose is a symbol of love. (*Bride's name*) and (*groom's name*), I ask that you exchange the roses you now hold.

If there is anything you remember and hold dear of this ceremony today, may it be that the blessing of God's love has brought you here to this garden ceremony; it is love that will make your marriage a glorious experience, and the continued sharing of your love for one another will sustain your marriage into the future.

(*Bride's name*) and (*groom's name*), press and dry your roses, and keep them in your family Bible as a place of safekeeping. When you gaze upon them in times to come, allow them to speak to your heart, saying to the other, "Thank you," "I'm sorry," "Happy Anniversary," and most importantly, "I love you today and always."

PRAYER OF BLESSING
To be offered at the conclusion of the wedding service, yet prior to the introduction of the couple:
May the grace of God fill your hearts with much love
    that your lives and marriage may grow and blossom.
May the light of Christ Jesus shine upon you. And,
    may the Spirit of God guide and nurture you for all
your days together.
Amen.

RENEWAL OF WEDDING VOWS

THEME

Love is often said to blossom and grow. As such, a peaceful garden setting is an appropriate venue to reaffirm a couple's wedding vows, celebrating how their love has grown and blossomed.

GREETING

Family members, friends, we are gathered together in the sight of God to witness and joyously bless the reaffirmation of the marriage covenant, first entered into by (*wife's name*) and (*husband's name*) _____ years ago.

Jesus, at a wedding in Cana of Galilee, gave us the example of the love to be shared by a husband and wife, and today we honor the love shared by (*husband's name*) and (*wife's name*) and celebrate the example they have shared with us.

GATHERING PRAYER

Loving God, Creator of us all,
>from our genesis in a garden setting,
>you have willed our lives to grow and blossom in
love.
>We ask once again your blessing on (*wife's name*) and
(*husband's name*)
>as they stand in this garden today to reaffirm the vows
they made _____ years ago.
>May our participation in the service of reaffirmation
>give us a renewed sense of faith, hope, and love.
>Allow your Holy Spirit to dwell within them and in us,
>as we are once again witnesses to their joy and peace.
>Continue to nourish and sustain their love. Amen.

MEDITATION

(*Wife's name*) and (*husband's name*), your lives have been
intertwined in marriage for _____ years now. I see signs of
this intertwining in several of the vines that grow in this
garden; some branches of the vine provide support for others, while some seek support and strength from others close
by. A marriage is a lot like these vines. For a marriage to last
as yours has, it is necessary to provide strength for each
other at times, and at other times, you will feel the need for
support and encouragement from the other.

(*Wife's name*) and (*husband's name*), it is apparent that you
have both attained a level of trust, freedom, and compassion that has allowed your love and your marriage to grow
and blossom in wonderfully joyous and meaningful ways.
In your growing together, you have nurtured that which is
good, healthy, and fruitful. You have successfully main-
tained and nurtured the garden of your love, and today,
we who have gathered with you on this significant occasion have all learned from your example. Not only have
you successfully nurtured your marriage but you have
also, knowingly or unknowingly, served to groom our

lives as well. We honor you for that influence you have blessed us with.

Your lives and your home have been much like a garden in which there has been a joyous harvest. You have enjoyed the fruits of your labor and have shared in the harvest that has allowed others to be nurtured and fed—spiritually, emotionally, and physically.

May our God of Creation continue to bless your lives as you serve together as "gardeners" in faith, hope, and love. Thanks be to God for the blessing of your lives.

REAFFIRMATION OF THE MARRIAGE COVENANT

(*Wife's name*) and (*husband's name*), ____ years ago you vowed your love for one another, and today you stand before God and this gathering to reaffirm those sacred vows.

(*Wife's name*), please repeat after me:
In the name of God, and with a thankful heart,
I, (*wife's name*), once again take you, (*husband's name*),
    as the love and joy of my life.
I promise to share times of laughter with you,
    grieve with you when necessary,
    and grow even more deeply in love with you.
I continue to offer to you my trust and respect in all ways possible.
You are truly my love, and today I honor you, and
    I am honored to be a part of your life, forever.

(*Husband's name*), please repeat after me:
In the name of God, and with a thankful heart,
I, (*husband's name*), once again take you, (*wife's name*),
    as the love and joy of my life.
I promise to share times of laughter with you,
    grieve with you when necessary,
    and grow even more deeply in love with you.

I continue to offer to you my trust and respect in all
ways possible.
You are truly my love, and today I honor you and
I am also honored to be a part of your life, forever.

PRAYER OF THANKSGIVING

Eternal God, Creator of all that is good,
provider of amazing grace, and giver of eternal love:
Bless and sanctify with your Holy Spirit
(*Wife's name*) and (*husband's name*)
who have this day reaffirmed their marriage covenant.
Allow them to continue to grow in love,
blossom in fruitfulness, and share their example
before others;
through Christ Jesus our Lord and Savior. Amen.

DISMISSAL WITH BLESSING

Throughout the years of your marriage,
God has attended to your needs,
the love of Christ has surely surrounded you, and
the presence of the Holy Spirit has guided you
to live in faith, hope, and love.
May you love continue to grow and blossom
and be fruitful in the eyes of our God. Amen.

INTRODUCTION OF COUPLE

Let us once again greet (*husband's name*) and (*wife's name*)
who have renewed and reaffirmed their commitment to
love and care for one another in the years ahead.

MEMORIAL SERVICE

THEME

The garden serves as a sacred vessel of memory for those departed souls so near and dear to our hearts.

GREETING

We have gathered in this memorial garden, in God's loving presence, to witness to our faith and to celebrate the life of (*deceased's name*) and to commend her/his soul into the eternal care of our Lord. We mourn our loss, yet we are also grateful for a life that has been lived and the memories of one we love and hold so dear.

Today, our tears will flow and mingle with those of God. By Christ's resurrection, we have been given the assurance of eternal life. Through the blessings of God, we hope to experience comfort in our celebration of (*deceased's name*) life, and we pray that we may find hope, peace, and promise in God's assurances.

GATHERING PRAYER

Lord, in our sorrow, we pray that you would wipe away our tears and bring us into closer fellowship with you. We are truly thankful for the love and joy that was shared with us through the life of (*deceased's name*). Our lives were truly enriched by his/her presence, and our faith increased by her/his wisdom and compassion.

We feel a great sense of loss and turn to you, Lord, for comfort. Help us each to be strong as we journey through the shadow-filled days that lie before us. May we experience the light and love of your eternal embrace.

You have promised to make all things new, so we pray that as you have called (*deceased's name*) to new life with you, that you would also renew us that we too might have hope and promise for the future.

We pray this in the name of the One who died our death, rose for our sake, and who will come again in glory. Amen.

SCRIPTURE READING
1 CORINTHIANS 15:35-38 (*THE MESSAGE*)

Some skeptic is sure to ask, "Show me how resurrection works. Give me a diagram; draw me a picture. What does this 'resurrection body' look like?" If you look at this question closely, you realize how absurd it is. There are no diagrams for this sort of thing. We do have a parallel experience in gardening. You plant a "dead" seed; soon there is a flourishing plant. There is no visual likeness between seed and plant. You could never guess what a tomato would look like by looking at a tomato seed. What we plant in the soil and what grows out of it don't look anything alike. The dead body that we bury in the ground and the resurrection body that comes from it will be dramatically different.

MEDITATION

We gather in memory today. We come together as family and friends to say good-bye to a loved one. We are here in the presence of God, who cares for us and provides even beyond what we have the strength and power and wisdom to fully grasp.

The Scripture that was read earlier is God's Word given to assure us that absent from the body, we are present with the Lord. That is, through the death and resurrection of Jesus, death has lost its sting, and death no longer has dominion over us. God has created us for immortality. In a comforting way, it can be said that God has done more than simply promise us a cure for disease; God has guaranteed us a cure for death.

In affirming this truth, the Apostle Paul compares the resurrection of the body to the growth of a plant from seed. A seed planted in the ground eventually grows and blossoms with new life. That is how it is when we die in Christ; we blossom into a new heavenly creation.

In the ritual of committal, we commend the deceased in sure and certain hope of resurrection to eternal life. Committing the body, ashes or remains "to the ground; earth to earth, ashes to ashes, dust to dust," is our final preparation for new life with Christ. For a Christian, at the very moment of death, the soul and the spirit go to be with God.

The Bible is quite clear that when God created human beings, it was not with the intention that the body was meant to die and decay in the ground. Rather, God created us to live forever, body and soul. However, our heavenly bodies will be transformed into something new, something much better.

Most every one of us has a certain level of uneasiness about change. But I believe the change we experience in being born anew into Heaven's realm is a change for the better; it will be so much more glorious and splendid and imperishable. When we die, like (*deceased's name*) has died, we will find ourselves alive in Christ Jesus.

Jesus has said, "Peace I leave with you, my peace I give to you," and "do not let your hearts be troubled and do not be afraid" (John 14:27 NIV). Fear not, family and friends, for our loved one now dwells in the Spirit of God.

WORDS OF COMFORT
This is an appropriate time to share words of the divine Shepherd as found in Psalm 23.

PRAYER OF THANKSGIVING
God, our Creator and Savior, we thank you for the gift of your Son, Jesus, who suffered, died, and was raised by you that we might come to know the fullness of risen life. We feel the loneliness and sadness of loss this day, and we turn to you for comfort. In our grief, we cannot help but to also rejoice that a life has been lived and has now been reborn into Heaven's realm. We praise you for (deceased's name) whom you have graciously received into your presence.

Enable us, Lord, to see beyond the mortal things of this world, to the wonderful promise of the eternal, as we await that glorious day when we all come together in a resurrection garden. In Jesus' name we pray. Amen.

BENEDICTION
As you leave this garden of memories,
    may God grant you peace.
May your lives be filled with hope,
    your hearts be flowing with promise,
    and may you always dwell in God's presence.
Go now in peace. Amen.

GRAVESIDE COMMITTAL SERVICE

There are those times when the family of a deceased person prefers not to host a traditional viewing and funeral, but opts for a simple, intimate graveside service. More frequently, the graveside service entails the burial of cremation remains rather than a casket.

THEME
Creation was experienced in a garden setting; so, too, our sorrowful good-byes often take place in a garden.

GREETING
Jesus said to her, "I am the resurrection and I am life. Those who believe in me, even though they die, will live, and everyone who lives and believes in me will never die" (John 11:25-26a). And he proclaimed, "I am the Alpha and the Omega, the Beginning and the End"; "I was dead, and behold I am alive forever and ever! And I hold the keys of death and Hades"; and "Because I live, you also will live" (Revelation 21:6; 1:18; John 14:19 NIV).

GATHERING PRAYER

Lord God, Creator of heaven and earth,
    we gather in sorrow this day, mourning our loss,
    yet thankful for the time we have spent together.
We give thanks for (*deceased's name*) life, and now we must
    commend him/her to your loving care.
We pray that you would raise him/her to new life in
your kingdom,
    that you would raise us, too, from death to life.
Grant, O God, that we may come to live with you and all
    whom we love, in your heavenly realm. Amen.

SCRIPTURE READING
ROMANS 6:3-11 (*THE MESSAGE*)

A reading from Paul's Letter to the Romans, chapter 6,
verses 3 through 11.

That is what happened in baptism. When we went
under the water, we left the old country of sin behind;
when we came up out of the water, we entered into the
new country of grace—a new life in a new land!

That's what baptism into the life of Jesus means. When
we are lowered into the water, it is like the burial of Jesus;
when we are raised up out of the water, it is like the resurrection of Jesus. Each of us is raised into a light-filled
world by our Father so that we can see where we're going
in our new grace-sovereign country.

Could it be any clearer? Our old way of life was nailed
to the cross with Christ, a decisive end to that sin-
miserable life—no longer at sin's every beck and call! What
we believe is this: If we get included in Christ's sin-
conquering death, we also get included in his life-saving
resurrection. We know that when Jesus was raised from
the dead it was a signal of the end of death-as-the-end.
Never again will death have the last word. When Jesus
died, he took sin down with him, but alive he brings God
down to us. From now on, think of it this way: Sin speaks a

dead language that means nothing to you; God speaks your mother tongue, and you hang on every word. You are dead to sin and alive to God. That's what Jesus did.

MEDITATION

We gather in memory this day. Here, in this garden of memories, we bury one we have loved so dearly. Today is a new day for (*deceased's name*) as he/she in now alive in Christ in heaven's garden. We come together to say good-bye to a loved one, but we also gather in the presence of a God who cares deeply for us, and Jesus tells us time and again—in both words and actions—that God does provide even beyond what we have the strength and power to understand until it happens.

The scripture reading from Paul's Letter to the Romans assures us that death no longer has the last word. As Jesus was nailed to that terrible cross, he took all the sins of the world upon his shoulders and carried them to the grave. In that decisive action, we are given the assurance that we are to be included in a life-saving resurrection. Each of us, who die in Christ, who are included in Christ's sin-conquering death, will be raised to a light-filled world where God will speak to us, comfort us, and wrap us in the arms of his love and compassion.

God's garden is a place of healing, reconciliation, and renewal. Today, (*deceased's name*) has been completely healed—body, mind, and spirit—and is enjoying new life in Christ. Today, (*deceased's name*) is counted among the angels in God's heavenly paradise.

Following his death, Jesus' lifeless body was buried in a garden tomb. From time to time, family members, loved ones, and friends will visit this garden to pay their respects. In that visit, recollections of times spent with (*deceased's name*) will surely come to mind. Each of us will remember (*deceased's name*) in our own special way. Preserve these memories, as they are what truly bind us together as family and as community.

WORDS OF COMFORT

Some of the most comforting words in Scripture are voiced in David's Psalm of the Divine Shepherd—the Twenty-third Psalm.

PRAYER OF COMMITTAL

Eternal God, into the loving arms of your embrace,
   and grateful for the promise of eternal life given
through Christ Jesus,
   we commit your servant, (*deceased's name*).
These remains (*this body*), we return to the ground,
   earth to earth, ashes to ashes, dust to dust.
Blessed are those who now rest from their labors.
Let us pray:
Gracious God, we give thanks for the gift of those we
love but see no more.
   We thank you that your love never ceases.
Receive (*deceased's name*) into your kingdom of love and
healing,
   and may he/she continue in service to you in your
heavenly kingdom. Amen.

BENEDICTION

As we leave this garden of memories,
   let us journey forth in the assurance of eternal life,
   and that we shall meet again one day,
   in that heavenly garden that surrounds the throne of
God.
   Go now in peace. Amen.

LITURGICAL GARDENS:
A RATIONALE

Since the beginning of time, the garden has been central to the human search for spiritual fulfillment and the discovery of inner peace and tranquility. For many religious traditions, the garden has emerged as that sacred place of sanctuary where one may connect with one's own soul and experience a Creator-God-Divine power though simple acts of prayer, meditation, or contemplation.

References to gardens as oases of comfort or as a symbol of paradise or heaven are found in much of the sacred literature of major religious traditions. Human beings continue to search for that idea of a lost paradise.

In many religious traditions, the garden is revered as a sacred place, ideal for establishing a greater connection with one's spirit or inner being. It is truly in the garden that one is able to experience an increased sense of peace and comfort through the holy acts of prayer, dialogue, and relaxation. The tasks of prayer, meditation, and contemplation become easier and more manageable in a comfortable setting that provides a sense of connection, not only to one's inner being but also, and more importantly, to a greater power, a creating and holy power.

> The many and great gardens of the world, of literature and poetry, of painting and music, of religion and architecture, all make the point as clear as possible. The soul cannot thrive in the absence of a garden. If you don't want paradise, you are not human; and if you are not human, you don't have a soul.[9]

The church, or other significant religious institution, has traditionally served as the locus in the community around which a diverse mix of people has gathered in prayer and worship. The building itself has typically functioned as a place of sanctuary where one may seek solace and comfort, set apart from the distractions and intrusions of the world. Such roots are found in the way the medieval cathedral builders sought to depict or convey a sense of heaven on earth within the walls of these grand structures. It is, however, in a liturgical garden where a person's spiritual, cultural, health, and emotional needs may be met in a simple, comfortable setting.

As such, the garden can, in a very unique and positive way, function as a bridge between various religious groups, traditions, and cultures. And it is in the garden that one begins to truly discover and experience something far greater than one's self.

Liturgical gardens, as a component of the overall institution's development scheme, can greatly aid in enhancing one's spiritual journey and the overall healing process. Viewing nature and relaxing in a comfortable outdoor environment is believed to enhance the healing process. When a person allows the many stresses of life to become overwhelming, the body's immune system makes one even more vulnerable to illness and infection. Striving for peace and contentment, especially by means of a garden setting, allows the body to return to near-peak performance levels, thereby maintaining a greater sense of health and wellness. Emotional, spiritual, and physical healing then becomes one of the key benefits of time spent in a garden engaged in prayer, meditation, or contemplation.

Gardens are indeed soothing to the soul and a source of refreshment to the body and mind. Garden-based experiences serve to facilitate contentment, peace, inner harmony, and tranquility. Human beings have long sought to create sacred spaces that are reminiscent of heaven or paradise: spaces that draw one closer to a Divine presence in nature and instill a greater sense of wonder and awe in the human species. Renowned landscape historian Derek Clifford describes this on-going human search:

> These sensations have led men to worship the genius of place from which it emanated. To such spots, men return again and again, ostensibly to please the Spirit with offerings, but really in order to enjoy the sensation dwarfing yet ennobling, not unlike the homes of the great deities, but every small stream became, in time, the manifestation of a nymph and every tree a resident dryad. Where this spirit was alive in the garden was not only a sanctuary but also the temple for the gods. The two emotions, joy in relief from stress and hunger for spiritual awakening, are the remote sources for leisured man's garden-making.[10]

Gardens certainly act as centering devices that allow for a cleansing of the mind, thereby facilitating a sense of not only emotional or physical healing but also a positive spirit of re-connection to a greater power, a holy and sacred divine power. A refreshed and rejuvenated spirit is genuinely beneficial for body and soul.

As one is re-connected, re-awakened, and re-energized by engaging in and experiencing a sacred and holy dialogue in a garden setting, the sense of wonder and awe and the sense of a more meaningful and satisfied life increase immeasurably.

> We can experience a natural religion removed from human dogma, conflict, or argument. Benches become pews, trees become

preachers, water becomes soulful baptisms, and choirs of flowers sing in great joy to the wind's organ voice.[11]

The overall significance of gardens is common to many religious traditions, from the Garden of Eden in the Old Testament and Tanakh of the Jewish faith to the Koran's representations of Paradise as a heavenly garden. Buddhists too have embraced the concept of creating gardens as places for spiritual meditation and contemplation. A liturgical garden, in a symbolic way, naturally functions as that common denominator or structure that bridges the many and diverse cultures and religion traditions present in the world.

Within the garden setting, especially a garden planned and formed as an integral component of a religious institution, it is possible to provide a positive venue for the conduct of liturgical rites and rituals. Gardens fashioned in such a unique and wonderfully calming environment provide a much-needed escape from the rigors of daily life.

In facilitating one's connection to the divine in a liturgical garden setting, an enhanced sense of hospitality is also extended to the user. It is in this generous gift of welcome and acceptance that the individual may be encouraged to visit the church and become a part of the worshiping community, thereby offering an even greater connection to the divine power being sought. In essence, the liturgical or prayer garden may provide a new and unique gateway to a more active and dynamic religious experience.

Not only does the prayer/liturgical garden facilitate one's spiritual journey but it also serves as a means of outreach, even if in somewhat of a covert manner. For some people, walking or even driving by may be the only contact they have with the religious building. What image people perceive of the grounds surrounding the building is certainly reflective of the quality of the interior. The garden, when well-planned and executed, becomes a rather dynamic invitation to participate in the life and liturgy of the worshiping community. The garden proudly and boldly speaks of invitation and hospitality; it is a powerful statement to the broader community that, in essence, says, "We are home, we are alive, we are active, and we welcome you!"

As our communities become more and more populated, as towns and suburbs are increasingly paved over with impervious cover, as more and more of the natural world is transformed into large-scale residential developments, strip malls and other commercial enterprises and other urbanized land uses, as nature is being ravaged on a daily basis, the need to create sacred natural spaces in a quiet, relaxed atmosphere becomes increasingly acute.

Liturgical gardens and other sacred, natural spaces serve as places of sanctuary to accommodate the rituals and practices of our personal and corporate spiritual disciplines. Gardens developed as a component of a religious facility's campus may serve a variety of functions. Not only is the liturgical garden a place for soul work and meditation but it also has the potential to function as an outdoor teaching and worship area, small group meeting place, and a joyous vessel for fellowship activities. Simple or elaborate in design, the cost of development is money and/or time well-spent in terms of human enrichment, enhancement, and enchantment.

There is a need for churches to add prayer/liturgical gardens to their setting. The result will provide a place of sanctuary for worship, prayer and meditation, for the greater community. Although with slightly a different meaning, my friend Leonard Sweet has urged, "Let's get the church out-of-doors!"

NOTES

1. C. A. Lowry, J. H. Hollis, A. de vries, B. Pana, L. R. Brunet, J. R. F. Hunt, J. F. R. Paton, E. van Kampen, D. M. Knight, A. K. Evans, G. A. W. Rook, and S. L. Lightman, "Identification of an Immune-responsive Mesolimbocortical Serotonergic System: Potential Role in Regulation of Emotional Behaviour," Neuroscience, 146 (28 March 2007), 756–72.

2. Leonard Sweet, "The 10 Commandments of Soulistic Health: Architecture for the Postmodern Reformation," in *Soul Café*, 1998, Vol. 1, No. 5-6, 7-8.

3. Thomas Moore, *The Re-Enchantment of Everyday Life* (New York: HarperCollins, 1966), 102.

4. J. Wayne Pratt, *Sanctuary: Prayers from the Garden* (Emunclaw, WA: PleasantWord, 2004), 7-8.

5. Moore, *Re-Enchantment of Everyday Life*, 97.

6. Roger S. Ulrich. "Evidence-based Garden Design for Improving Health Outcomes." *Investigating the Relationship Between Health and the Landscape: Therapeutic Conference Report.* University of Minnesota Landscape Arboretum, 2000.

7. Robert Schuller, quoting architect Richard Neutra. "Physical Environment Shapes Our Transcendence." The AIA Journal of Architecture. December, 2005. <http://aia.org/nwslter_aiaj.cfm?pagename+aiaj_a-20050730_biorealism>. (Accessed 13 April 2009).

8. The image of God as "Master Gardener" is dramatically highlighted in Eugene Peterson's paraphrase, *The Message: The Bible in Contemporary Language*.

9. Moore, *Re-Enchantment of Everyday Life*, 101.

10. Derek Clifford, *The History of Garden Design* (New York: Praeger, 1967), 24.

11. Christopher Forrest McDowell and Tricia Clark McDowell, *The Sanctuary Garden: Creating a Place of Refuge in Your Yard or Garden* (New York: Simon & Schuster (A Fireside Book), 1998), 20.

CPSIA information can be obtained at www.ICGtesting.com
Printed in the USA
LVOW011025170113

315851LV00003B/4/P